How to Get the Ring On Your Finger

By Cezanne Poetess

(with Contributions from over 30 Brothers)

ISBN: 978-0-9576969-4-5

Email: artisanimpression@gmail.com

How to Get The Ring On Your Finger

CONTENTS

Dedication

To and for all my single sisters who inspired me to write this book, and for the Kings who are waiting to meet their Queens – We Belong Together!

Introduction

Are you a Single Woman of African descent seeking to meet and marry your Soul Mate?

Have you done everything the 'right way', and are wondering why you STILL haven't attracted the 'right man' to settle down with?

Are you concerned that you may reach menopause and lose out on the possibility of having a baby?

Do you want to get to the bottom of your relationship issues so you can heal your Self and best prepare your Self to meet your match?

This book is for YOU!

I was inspired to write this book while taking part in a BHM exhibition in October 2013. At the exhibition I met yet another Black sister in her mid forties who felt she might have left it too late to start a family while waiting for 'Mr Right'. Many of such sisters are concerned about reaching menopause childless, and are faced with making the difficult decision of having a baby regardless of whether the man is going to be a supportive father or not. This is a difficult predicament to find yourself in if you *want* children. Then there are many single sisters who *have* children who are also looking to meet someone to settle down with.

And of course this isn't all one-sided; there are many single Black men waiting to meet their soul mate too.

So I asked my Higher Self to help *me* help *you* to attract and marry your soul mate. I was instructed to write this book, and to ask the brothers – both married and single – to give their advice on how a sister should conduct herself during the dating process for a better chance of *marriage*; the question I posed was **"What advice can you give to our sisters who are seeking to meet and marry**

a Good Black Man (or to get their man to commit?)/ What would make YOU want to put a ring on a woman's finger?"

Within three weeks I had enough material to put this book together, including all the images! Over 30 men were eager to contribute to this book, and it is an insightful look into why our (Black) relationships are the way they are, and what we can do to heal ourselves.

Even though it was Black History Month and I was involved in a lot of events, I was still able to put it all together within six weeks. The inspiration was flowing!

Throughout this book, I'm going to help you (with the help our brothers and my Higher Self) to Attract Your Soul Mate and Keep Him – for as long as it serves you both. It is NOT meant to be a step-by-step manual, but more of a guide to give you the best chances of getting the ring on your finger.

Ladies....over 30 brothers have taken the time to sit down, think, and make a POSITIVE CONTRIBUTION to this book so SSSSHHHHHHHH....listen carefully to what they have to say!

(I've put all the links to where you can find out more about the brothers who have contributed to this book at the BACK, so you don't get distracted looking at their profiles – read the book first!)

I used my painting *'Love Bump'* to illustrate the front cover of this book because it perfectly illustrates what its book about. The painting didn't come *from* me, it came *through* me. Later on in the book we're going to do a Creative Visualisation Relaxation technique using *'Love Bump'* that will help you focus on your desires and get in the right vibration to attract your soul mate.

I'm not going to scare you with statistics about how many single Black women over 30 there are, or how many single Black men there are in ratio to the women or anything like that. The aim of this book is to help you attract your soul mate. You have to believe he's out there in order to be able to attract him!

Although this book is initially written for my single sisters, I advise that both parties (men and women) read it and follow 'the rules'. I didn't make them up. I write from my Higher Self, meaning I just write and let the words flow through me. I completed this book in 6 weeks from the initial idea, to receiving all the contributions, all the images and putting everything in order.

I hope you find the information in this book helpful, and that it will go some way to helping YOU meet and marry the right man for you! And if you're a man, visa versa – because I know you're going to want to read it too, which is good, as both parties need to be in agreement!

May this book help us find ourselves and each other – We Belong Together!

Cezanne

****

My Her-Story

You might be wondering what qualifies me to write this book since I've never been married myself, but I *have* been proposed to *3 times* (well one was more of an *indirect* proposal, but I'll tell you more about that later!). For now, I'll just say that it was my choice to remain unmarried. Why?

When I was growing up, marriage was never indoctrinated into me as much as the religion that supported it. I grew up in a single-parent household; my mother never married (although all her sisters did), and she never advised any of her children to get married before having children. Maybe she felt she wasn't in a position to. Yet even though I never married, I made sure I drummed 'marriage before children' into my two older son's heads when they were little; I wanted them to do better than their dad, and grow up to be responsible fathers committed to their children.

So I was never one of those little girls who dreamt of walking down the aisle in a white dress, going on honeymoon, and living happily ever after.

But I still managed to clock up three marriage proposals:

I met 'R' at the Notting Hill Carnival when I was 19 (He was 5 months older than me). Not actually *in* the Carnival, but at the end. Me and a girlfriend met up with some old school friends who offered to give us a lift home. 'R' turned up in his mum's car. I'd never met him before but he kept looking at me in his rear view mirror; he later told me that it was my eyes that caught his attention. Anyway, somehow he managed to make sure I was the last person to drop off, and we sat in the car and chatted. He invited me out the following weekend, and after a few dates asked *"Will you go out with me?"*

'R' was a real gem. A black pearl, so to speak. I mean, he really had his head screwed on the right way (unlike me). He was just beginning a career in IT, wasn't the type to play around, was handsome, smart, funny, and I learnt from his sister that I was the first Black girl he'd been out with. He fell head over heels in love with me, I could do no wrong in his eyes. But because I still had extreme Self-esteem issues, I couldn't see what he saw in *me*. I convinced myself that he was too good for me, and would disappear once he got what he wanted. So I made him wait. Three months.

But the longer I made him wait, the more he seemed to fall in love with me. By the end of the three months I had his heart in my hands.

Yet I was still thinking "He's going to change, he's too good to be true"

In the first year, I ended the relationship at least 10 times. 'R' was always the one to put it back together again.

Then for once, *he* ended it with *me*.

I was distraught; I have a vague recollection of chasing him through Finsbury Park calling out his name.

Later that morning, he dropped a letter through the door saying he'd only ended it so I could see what it felt like.

That's when I realised he wasn't going anywhere.

So I settled into the relationship and I honestly couldn't have asked for a better boyfriend. He even let me practice my barbering skills on his head. I remember accidentally shaving a patch in his head while talking to his friend, and he *still* let me carry on practicing on him until I got good at it. I saved a lot of money later on when I had my two boys.

When I got my first job working for an Insurance Brokers 'R' took me shopping and bought me a brand new red coat and a matching red and black briefcase. And when he started a new IT job I bought him colourful shirts and ties with matching socks.

We were 'made for each other'. People always commented on how good we looked together.

When we were 21 'R' proposed. He gave me three weeks to give him an answer. I waited until the last day of the 3 weeks and then said "Yes".

'R' was over the moon; he carved on the side of his bedside table 'Carol Ann said yes!' (my old name)

But the idea of marriage didn't really appeal to me. It felt like a life sentence.

I couldn't go through with the marriage even though I *did* get the ring on my finger.

Instead, 5 years later I got pregnant for a man who didn't give two hoots about me. A classic case of Self-sabotage, don't you think?

'R' has now been happily married for over 20 years.

Yes that could have been me.

But *should* it have been? No.

The second proposal was from my youngest son's father. In fact, I don't remember him proposing, but I do remember him taking me shopping to buy the ring.

Most women in the position I was in at the time would have been happy and content;

We were living in a 5 bedroom house with a garden the size of a football pitch. He had taken my two older boys on as his own, I didn't have to do the 9-5; My days were taken up doing housework, looking after the baby, doing the school run, ironing his shirts for work, cooking dinner etc.

If I was 'wifey material' I would have been content, but instead, I kept thinking "This is not my life!"

I felt like a caged bird. When my youngest son was a year old I wrote his dad this poem:

'Not Just a MUM'

(Expressions of a Frustrated Housewife)

"I'm not just a 'MUM' –
I have a life outside the home!
I've spent the last umpteen years
Washing, cooking, cleaning, ironing,
Changing baby's padding,

Nursing, dressing, school-running
Never ending house-working!

I 'work' 16 hours a day AT LEAST
So why aren't I entitled to a Lunch Break,
Free Weekends or Annual Leave?

Why don't you take the job I do at home seriously?
Don't tell me 'I've got it easy'
I sacrificed <u>my</u> career to have <u>your</u> baby
And you don't even appreciate me
OR what I do for this family!

Child rearing is the hardest job ever made –
And I don't even get paid!

So don't ask me what I do in the house all day,
And don't belittle me
Just because I don't bring home a wage;

Let me take just ONE DAY OFF
And you'll see what'll become of this place!

If you didn't have me,
You'd have to pay a nanny to look after the baby,
A maid to keep this house clean and tidy,
A cook to prepare your meals,
So that after your 'hard day at work'
your food is on the table, ready
And an accountant to s-t-r-e-t-c-h your money:

What, did you think it got done all by itself?
And after MY hard day of work,
I don't even get time to my Self!

I work as day nurse, night nurse, story-teller
Chauffeur, teacher, first-aider,
Chancellor of our bank-chequer,

House maintainer, home-maker!

I'm on call 24 hours a day with our cuties,
Not to mention performing my 'wifely duties'

So why do you begrudge me
taking 'Time Out' to my Self?
And why are you always 'too tired' to help?
Do you think you do more work than me
Just because YOU bring in the money?

I NEED TIME OUT!

So when I want to go out dancing
Relaxing, or no-kids shopping
Don't cage me in
For like a bird I must fly,
To my nest always returning.

I'm NOT just a mum;
I'm a writer, an artist, an actor, a dancer
A friend, a sister, an aunt, a godmother!
And no more will these parts of me be suppressed –
(inhales deeply)
Well, I'm glad I got that all off my chest!"
© Cezanne Poetess 2005

A year later I 'flew the nest'. The housewife role just didn't agree with me.

The third proposal was *indirect*, however it came from 'the man of my dreams' (the guy I based the 'Charles' character on in my Self-help novel *'Single, Spiritual…AND Sexual!'*)

The day we first met, time literally stood still. I'd never felt anything like it before. In fact, the way the two main characters met in **Year One** of my novel is exactly the way *we* met; I was doing my very first stand at an event in 2001 and I spotted him from across the crowded room. A strange feeling came over me, as if I knew him, yet we'd never met before (in this lifetime).

8

When he finally reached my stand, we both experienced a 'twilight zone' moment. In fact, when I emailed him the first chapter of the book in 2010, he called early the following morning to give me *his* version of the encounter, telling me to throw it in randomly somewhere in the story, but *not* in Year One, which is exactly what I did! (You can find it in **Year Five** – don't spoil it for yourself by jumping ahead though!). Now after reading his version of the account you're probably going to want to know why we're not together; well to cut a long story short, we grew apart: In between our 'encounters' I had my third son – not for him (he's still unmarried with no children).

In 2007 we were talking on the phone and he said "I think you'd be very happy married to me". Now this might sound a bit arrogant but you've got to understand, this was coming from 'the man of my dreams' so to speak. Plus, he was financially stable; he had properties, a Mercedes convertible (in fact he had two cars), a well-paid job, he was tall, good-looking, and was the type of man who wouldn't stray once he's committed to you. He was 'husband material'.

Instead of me replying with what any woman who was dying to get the ring on her finger might say, e.g. "Are you proposing?" I replied "What makes you think that??"

Now you might not think that this counts as a marriage proposal, but even though I didn't get a ring from 'H', he did question me a couple of times as to why I wear a ring on my wedding finger. He would look at it in the way Charles looked at the cross around Suzanne's neck in **Year One** of my novel (FREE to read by the way!). Most women who are looking to get a ring on their finger would have removed it quick time, but not me.

I still wear a ring on my wedding finger. It's not a wedding ring, it's more of a sign to say 'I'm not available for marriage'.

So there you have it, three proposals. Three opportunities to be somebody's wife.

Now I see why my friend Bunmi nicknamed me 'the runaway bride'. He used to joke and say he could just picture me galloping off into the sunset on a horse in my wedding dress. He told me I was afraid of commitment. My middle son said the same thing, saying I should marry 'H' (after all, he was the only man my sons saw keep coming in and out of my life over the years).

But for me, there was 'more to life' than being a wife. I had my three sons 'out of wedlock' – all unplanned pregnancies. Even now I find it hard to believe I'm a mother to three young men; my eldest is now 21, my middle son is 18 and my youngest is 9.

In 2008 when my youngest son 'Azzy' was four years old I sent him to live with his father (and my two older boys to live with *their* dad). For the first time in years I was able to focus on ME. I learnt how to meditate, painted 11 paintings, had my first exhibition, wrote and recorded numerous poems, 13 of which are on my first poetry CD *'Seeds of Love'* (I also produced the CD), and wrote my first novel. It was only when I started writing the novel that I realised my artwork and poetry could be used to illustrate it, so that's what I did!

I've also written and recorded 9 more poems towards my next CD *'Rise of the Phoenix'*, and now *this* book. I've written scripts, built websites, and worked on developing my *mind*. Not many people know this, but I did all the formatting and design for my Self-help novel, my poetry CD *and* its Book of Lyrics. On one occasion I sat for 15 hours figuring out how to format the novel so I could get the chapters to say 'Year One, Year Two, Year Three...' on one side, and the title of the book on the other. It took *intense focus*.

I know that if I had been in a relationship I wouldn't have got so much work done. I pray for the day when I meet someone who can actually *help* me with my work. But up to this point, I've enjoyed having time to focus on my Self and doing what I love – being creative!

Anyway, I now feel ready to settle down again, so we're going to do this together – the only difference is you'll be looking to attract a *husband*, whereas I'll be looking to attract a *life partner* – my Soul Mate.

What is a 'Soul Mate', and How Will You Know When You've Found Yours?

♥ A person ideally suited to another as a close friend or romantic partner.

♥ A person with whom one has a feeling of deep or natural affinity. This may involve similarity, love, sexuality/sexual activity, spirituality, or compatibility and trust

♥ A person with whom you have an immediate connection the moment you meet – a connection so strong that you are drawn to them in a way you have never experienced before. As this connection develops over time, you experience a love so deep, strong and complex, that you begin to doubt that you have ever truly loved anyone prior. Your soul mate understands and connects with you in every way and on every level, which brings a sense of peace, calmness and happiness when you are around them. And when you are not around them, you are all that much more aware of the harshness of life, and how bonding with another person in this way is the most significant and satisfying thing you will experience in your lifetime. You are also all that much aware of the beauty in life, because you have been given a great gift and will always be thankful.

♥ Your soul mate is the 'other you'. This will be the one you spend the rest of your life loving, and getting to know. You will still argue and fight, but you will also complete each other's sentences and instinctively understand the others feelings. This is the person you look for all your life, and no matter when you find them, they are always worth the wait.

(I got all those answers from the internet).

Can You Have More Than One Soul Mate?

I believe it IS possible to have more than one soul mate. Don't get hung up on the guy you had a real connection with. He's gone. He served his purpose. Relationships don't *have* to last a lifetime, they are there to help you *grow* and *develop*. If you're in a relationship that's keeping you from growing, it's unhealthy. Don't stay in a relationship just so you can say you're in one. I'm not promoting promiscuity; in fact I haven't had sex since my last encounter with 'H'. Each encounter with him helped me grow in some way (I'd like to think it did the same for him). Over the years though, we evolved into two very different types of people. If we *had* got married, one of us would have been miserable, and it wouldn't have been me.

'T' was my soul mate too. I lived with him for two years during a period of 'homelessness'. It was during this period that I did my paintings, learnt how to meditate, and we even worked on the *'Seeds of Love'* project together. I decided to write lyrics to his beautifully inspired music captured on his Dictaphone. I downloaded them to the computer, listened to them over and over again until I was inspired to write words to go with them (I wrote 11 poemsongs to his music in total, some will be on my *next* CD).

'T' served me well. He cooked, cleaned, gave me my space (even though it was his flat) and generally nurtured me. That's what I needed *at that time*. He would run the bath for me, massage my body, wash my underwear by hand, and generally make sure that I was free to be me. He admired me. He enjoyed watching me paint. We co-created together. But I knew he wasn't going to be the one I could 'build empires with'. I needed someone who was going to be stronger than me mentally.

But he was right for me *at that time*.

Are Soul Mates for Life?

I personally don't believe that relationships have to last 'forever'. I don't even think it's *healthy* to stay in a relationship if it's not helping you to grow as an individual. Oftentimes, two people cross paths on their individual journeys in life, and if they're not heading in the same direction, will later on find out that they are in two different places (destinations). Once you've learnt your 'lesson' from that relationship, it's time to move on. It is rare that you will meet your soul mate first time, get married and still be 'together' 30 years later. I'm still waiting to meet the man who is walking the same path as me and growing at the rate I'm growing; if you are not growing at the same rate, one of you will get left behind.

If you're stuck in a marriage (or relationship) that is stagnant, neither of you will be able to grow to your full potential. I've had some really beautiful, deep, meaningful relationships, but I have no desire to go back to them. They served their purpose and helped me to grow into the person I am today. You've got to know when it's time to move on. Have no fear! Something better is down the road...

Are You Afraid of Being Alone?

Before expecting someone to join you on *your* journey in life, you should have an idea of where you're going.

If you have not yet asked your Self the questions "Who Am I?" and "Why am I here?" you have not yet begun your journey of Self-discovery. Most people are frightened of spending time alone in the Silence. They'll have the tell-lie-vision on for company, or the radio, or they'll get on the phone and call a friend. Their own company just isn't good enough. When you begin your journey of Self-discovery you'll begin to *appreciate* your own company.

*"A goddess is a woman who emerges from deep within herself.
She is a woman who has honestly explored her darkness and
learned to celebrate her light. She is a woman who is able to fall
in love with the magnificent possibilities within her. She is a
woman who knows of the magic and mysterious places inside her,
the sacred places that can nurture her soul and make her whole"*
~ **Orman Griffith**

Take some time *today* to just sit in the Silence, on your own. Switch your phone off (or put it on silent if the thought of being totally phoneless is too much). Close your eyes. Take deep breaths and connect with your inner Self. Stay there. Don't start fidgeting and thinking that nothing's happening. Go deeper. Look deep inside your Self. It's only in the Silence that you can begin to hear your inner voice clearly, and connect with The Real You.

"Meditation is nothing but a time when you can relax utterly into yourself, when you close all your doors, all your senses, to the outside stimulus. You disappear from the world. You forget the world as if it exists no more – no newspapers, no radio, no television, no people. You are alone in your innermost being, relaxed, at home" ~ **Eye'm King**

Get to know your Self fully, before trying to get to know someone else. Who are you? What are you here for? What do you stand for? What are your dreams, goals and aspirations? Are you clear about your own life? Spend time alone, in the Silence, with a notebook and pen, and write down the answers to these questions. Are they clear to you?

What do you want out of life? Where do you see your Self in a year's time? Three years? Ten years? Before thinking about meeting and getting to know a man, get to know your Self first!

Know Your Worth

Some advice from the brothers about knowing your Self/your Worth:

"A Woman has to know her worth and she has to know what she will accept and not accept. A Woman also has to know that sometimes being alone and being married to her Self is one of the best relationships that she can ever be in. LOVE THY SELF. And when she is able to do that all things will come to her" ~ **Kushi Myers**

"First, know thyself (faith, values, beliefs). If you don't stand for something, you stand for nothing. Having a solid foundation will ensure you project outwards your needs...and attract the ideal person you deserve" ~ **LG** (Motivational Speaker and Success Coach)

"Know yourself. If you're insecure and you marry a secure man, no matter how much he affirms your beauty, his love for you etc. you will not be able to respond to his love and positive affirmations about you." ~ **Bunmi**

15

"Women who are seeking their ultimate eternal soul mate should really concentrate on knowing themselves. Knowing what they truly want in a relationship. Relationships are never going to be easy because we are forever changing beings. It's best to be always changing for the positive. Women should never use sex to get a man, they should use knowledge. Show respect for themselves. Not dress cheaply and tartishly."

~ **Yeshuah the 1st**, Conscious hip-hop rapper

Poem by Sojourner Truth: 'Ain't I A Woman'

"That man over there say a woman needs to be helped into
carriages and lifted over ditches
And to have the best place everywhere.
Nobody ever helped *me* into carriages or over mud puddles
or gives me a best place...
And ain't I a woman?
Look at me, look at my arm!
I have plowed and planted and gathered into barns,
and no man could head me...
And ain't I a woman?
I could work as much and eat as much as a man -
When I could get to it - And bear the lash as well.
And ain't I a woman?
I have borne 13 children and seen most sold into slavery
And when I cried a mother's grief
None but Jesus heard me...
And ain't I a woman?
That little man there in black say a woman can't have as much
rights as a man cause Christ wasn't a woman...
Where did your Christ come from?
From God and a woman!
Man had nothing to do with Him!
If the first woman God ever made was strong enough to turn the
world upside down,
All alone together women ought to be able to turn it
Right-side up again".

If an enslaved woman who's been raped, beaten, had her children sold into slavery, forced to serve a false god, and had all her dignity stripped from her can *still* realise her Self-worth, so can you.

Identify Your 'Issue'

I know what *my* issues are, do you?

I identified my issue as being 'emotionally unavailable', meaning I was out of touch with my feelings. In the past I could really be 'in love' with a brother, but wouldn't know how to express that to him verbally. I could have feelings deep enough to swim in, but the words just wouldn't come out of my mouth. I have sabotaged my best relationships because I didn't feel worthy of them.

I was finally able to get to the *root cause* of my issue a couple of years ago during my own Self-healing journey: when I was growing up, I never heard the words "I love you" from my mother (or father). I was never hugged, or treated in a loving way. I felt as if my mother didn't even *like* me, let alone *love* me. I grew up in fear of being attacked with the belt (or whatever else my mother could lay her hands on). I was told I'm the 'ugly duckling of the family' because I was the darkest of the daughters. I was told I was a 'whatless good-for-nothing croft'. The verbal abuse affected me worse than the physical abuse, because it affected me *psychologically*; I grew up believing I was ugly, worthless and unlovable.

I had to do a lot of work on my Self to get where I am now; with raised Self-esteem, learning to love my Self unconditionally and seeing that true beauty has nothing to do with the shade of my skin – in fact, now I wouldn't mind being darker, especially after learning about the benefits of Melanin!

If you were to meet me now, you wouldn't believe that some years ago I had low Self-esteem, and couldn't see what any man could possibly love about me. I didn't believe in my Self or my abilities and remained a blocked writer and artist for over 20 years. It took years of working with Positive Affirmations where I would look in the mirror and affirm to my Self things like *"I, Cezanne am a brilliant and successful artist, I am a prolific writer, I am a first-class performer, I am confident and competent in my creative work, I trust my perceptions, I love my Self, I feel good about my Self, I am beautiful...."* I still struggle with the last one, but I keep affirming it to my Self anyway. The great thing about working with Positive Affirmations is that eventually people begin telling you what you've been telling your Self, without them even knowing it. Do you know how many people have told me I am a goddess, or that I am beautiful, or a prolific writer? Your outer world is simply a reflection of your inner world! I am *still* working on my Self....

Until you are able to identify *why* you are still single, you won't be in a position to heal your Self. You could come up with all sorts of reasons why you are still single, like "there are not enough black men to go around", or "all the good Black men are already married", or "It's not ME with the issue, it's HIM!"

It's Time to Heal Our Selves!

Where do our relationship issues stem from? What is the ROOT CAUSE of our problems?

In order to go FORWARD we have to go BACK

I was inspired to write the poem '*We Belong Together*' after watching the film *'Sankofa'*; the film traumatized me but helped me realise that the root cause of our *current* relationship issues are rooted in our *past*:

*"First we have to understand our recent history; those of us taken from Africa to the Western hemisphere during the enslavement were not allowed to create a family. It is only in the last 175 years since Maafa that West Indians were allowed to create a family. Marriage before 50 is a new concept. It is unwise to compare ourselves to other groups of people; we are still practicing practices taught to us during slavery. Men had no rights over their children. This is **genetic memory**, it is **taught behaviour**. If we don't understand our history, we won't be able to understand why we behave the way we do, and consequently we won't be able to correct our behaviour. There are people who don't know that they don't know, and there are people who don't WANT to know. The reason we can't go forward is because we won't go backward"* ~ **Michael**, BIS Publications

In **Year Two** of my Self-help novel '*Single, Spiritual...AND Sexual!*' Suzanne was shocked when she began learning about what happened to her ancestors during their 400 years of enslavement; yet it helped her to innerstand her own 'Independent Black Woman' attitude, and why the father of her two children couldn't seem to help doing a disappearing act as soon as she got pregnant. It also helped her to change her own behavioural patterns and expect *marriage* before having any more children.

"We talk about our history and we talk about the experiences we've had; we have documentation about Willie Lynch and his psychological programming; well part of the psychological programming was to hang, draw and quarter the most strongest-looking Black man in order to traumatize the observers. Then they would get another strong-looking Black man and whip him to the end of his life – not to death, but until he became like a snivelling little youth getting terrorized by his mother. The women and children are observing this. The purpose of it is to traumatize the mind, so they could start moulding it the way they wanted it to be. This dropped the frequencies in the women by making them full of fear. Then they (the enslavers) would fight the resistance being put up by the women as if they were breaking in a horse, as they would say "whip her until all the bitchiness is beaten out of her". Now they could negotiate through her. She now looks up to the white man as the man (not the Black man), HE (the white man) now has all the masculine energy that she fears (not loves), and learns to respect him like the Stockholm Syndrome, and begins to friggin' love her own abuser. This is the psychology that you still see happening today between Black people. You mess with the root, you've got the whole tree" ~ **Siayoum Atum Ab Ankh Rhem**, Astrologer

Are the effects of slavery still affecting us today?

Michael Baisden Commentary: Worse Than Slavery

"I woke up in the middle of the night still troubled by the images I had seen in the movie, '12 Years A Slave'. I couldn't get the scene out of my mind of the families being torn apart and auctioned off to different plantations; mother and child and brother and sister never to see each other again. As my eyes slowly opened... slightly watery I played back the horrific sound of the slave masters whip as it tore the flesh off the black female character's back. The sight of the blood shooting profusely from her body made my blood boil. I was pissed!

But my anger wasn't only for the institution of slavery or the cruel slave masters that raped, tortured, and murdered our people, my disdain was focused mainly on those black and brown people who don't realize we are still enslaved...in many ways worse than legalized slavery.

Instead of black families being torn apart at the auction block, millions of black men and women voluntarily walk away from their children leaving them vulnerable to rape, molestation and imprisonment. There is no need for plantations where we pick cotton in the relentless summer heat, those industries have been replaced by "For Profit" prisons were the government pays corporate slave masters 60,000 a year to lock away poor black and brown people for many more years than whites for the same crime and then contract them out to other greedy corporations for higher profits.

So what's worse, a system of slavery where we are forced into violence, ignorance, and stabbing each other in the back, or a system where we voluntarily kill and betray one another, abandon our children, and refuse to read a book? You tell me!

What was most disturbing was that the story of Solomon Northup being kidnapped and sold into slavery was a true tale. He was one of many thousands, the majority of who would never see freedom or their families again. Most of them died breaking their backs eighteen hours a day in horrendous conditions. It took him 12 years in the worse conditions imaginable to finally make it home. But you and I have the freedom today to stop this madness and start working together as a people to improve our social and economic condition. But we seem unwilling or unable to do so, and to me, that's worse than slavery!

And we wonder why other races don't respect us. We waste our valuable resources trying to keep up with the Joneses, we as black men disrespect our women, in frustration our women shout, "I don't need a man!", we abandon our children out of selfishness,

21

and we refuse to pool our resources together and instead beg other races for employment and money to educate our children. That's worse than slavery!

I tried to go back to sleep but I was unable to. I couldn't help thinking about the nearly empty theater I sat in to watch this amazing film. With the exception of the people I invited, teacher Mr. Wheeler, and the 20 young men we mentor at Evans High School, the majority of people in attendance were white. How in the hell can we expect to move forward when we are too lazy or ashamed to acknowledge our own history and pay tribute to those who made it possible for us to be here? And that, to me, is worse than physical slavery; it's mental slavery! Wake up people, the fight is not over!"

Please Share This With All Your Friends! ~ **Michael Baisden**, Bestselling Author & Motivational Speaker

A Quick Our-Story Lesson:

'The majority of the records obtained from ships transporting captive Africans to Europe and the New world during the Trans-Atlantic Slave Trade identify their main source of human cargo as being from Senegal, Gambia, Ghana, Nigeria, Sierra Leone and Benin. The Akan of Western Africa make up one of the largest ethnic/cultural groups inhabiting Ghana and the Ivory Coast. A selection of the Akan as representative of early African slaves brought to the New World is arbitrary only insofar as historical evidence points towards the Western coast of Africa as the primary source of imported slaves.

The Akan have an ancient and rich cultural heritage that includes the extensive use of pictorial symbolism in the writing system known as **Adinkra,** which was created by the Ashanti craftsmen of Ghana. The Adinkra symbolize the Akan way of life, and individually each symbol can be associated with an **aphorism** or **proverb** rooted in the Akan experience. African proverbs offer insight into African philosophical thought, cosmology, and worldview, so that collectively, the Adinkra and their accompanying proverbs form a communication system that preserves and transmits the accumulated cultural and spiritual values of the people.

Sankofa is an Akan term that literally means, "to go back and get it." One of the Adinkra symbols for Sankofa (above) depicts a mythical bird flying forward with its head turned backward. The egg in its mouth represents the "gems" or knowledge of the past upon which wisdom is based; it also signifies **the generation to come** that would benefit from that wisdom. This symbol often is associated with the proverb, *"Se wo were fi na wosankofa a yenkyi,"* which translates to **"It is not wrong to go back for that which you have forgotten."** The Akan believe that the past illuminates the present and that the search for knowledge is a life-long process. The pictograph illustrates the quest for knowledge, while the proverb suggests the rightness of such a quest as long as it is based on knowledge of the past'.

(**SAN** = "to return") + (**KO** = "to go") + (**FA** = "to look, to seek and take")

'We must go back and reclaim our past so we can move forward; so we understand *why* and *how* we came to be who we are today.'

I wasn't even in a relationship when I wrote *'We Belong Together'*. The emotions I was feeling were as a result of watching the film *'Sankofa'* the night before. I dedicated it to all descendants of the enslaved still suffering from Post Traumatic Slave Syndrome:

> *Yeah I know sometimes I don't treat you right*
> *And I bet you wonder what happened to me*
> *Why I seem so uptight and angry?*

And all I wanna seem to do is fuss and fight
And not give you the right to take your place
As King upon your throne in our home

But sometimes I can't seem to help the way I feel,
It's like something that's been passed down to me through my
bloodline
And I need you to help me heal...

See, my brother, my King,
I'm beginning to innerstand
That I'm still in an emotional state of shock
After seeing the things they did to you in our history,
And the things they did to me!
So you see,
There's a lot of healing that needs to take place
between you and me,
And our community
And I'm willing to do whatever it takes to help us heal, are you?

Because brother, I want us to be together
I choose you, not another
And I'm trying, I'm really trying to heal
But you've got to help me, and I've got to help you
Brother, we need each other,
I can't do it without you, and you can't do it without me
We've got to stick together, We Belong Together

Let's not let another come between us,
Let the Love for each other be stronger

And I know sometimes I don't treat you right
And all I wanna seem to do is fuss and fight
And not give you the right to take your place
as King upon your throne in our home
But I can't do it without you, and you can't do it without me
See, we need each other
We've got to stick together, We Belong Together

Let's not let another come between us,
Let the Love for each other be stronger

My brother, my King,
We've got to do this together

(We've got to heal ourselves)

And I know sometimes I treat you like less than a man
And yes I know you have your own issues to deal with,
Lack of employment weighing you down
Disabling you from providing for me and our children
'cos that's the way they planned it,
So that I would not give you your rightful position as 'My King'
But I will do my best to help you in whatever way I can,
To help you rise and be the man you're destined to be, to me.

And there are times when I pretend I don't need you,
And you act like you don't want me
But the truth is,
I'm your sister, you're my brother
And we've got to stick together
We need each other,
We Belong Together.

Let's not let another come between us,
Let the Love for each other be stronger

And yeah, I know sometimes I verbally abuse you
Because there's so much pain inside of me
But today I pledge to do the best I can
To help you rise to be the man,
The KING you're destined to be.

© Cezanne Poetess 2011

Before Afrikans were enslaved by Europeans, the family was
the core of the community. The Black Woman was the nuclear of

that core, and it 'took a village to raise a child'. During their 400 years of enslavement, families were torn apart, the strongest men were publicly slaughtered and humiliated, the women were raped and turned into sex slaves (I dread to think that the children were too), they were stripped of their names, language, and spirituality and forced to worship a false god. If you have never read the Willie Lynch letter, I suggest you do, in order to fully realise that the *psychological* trauma our ancestors suffered was far worse than the *physical* trauma, because it's still affecting their descendants today.

Symptoms of Post Traumatic Slave Syndrome:

Do you look up to the white man while having little respect for the Black man? Do you have an 'I don't need a man' attitude? Do you allow others to abuse your body sexually? Do you still see the white Jesus as your god? Do you beat your children mercilessly? Do you wish you were white, or lighter skinned? These are just *some* of the psychological imprints of what was done to our ancestors, and handed down to you genetically. If you don't know where your behaviour comes from, you will not be in a position to begin the process of healing your Self.

Jada Pinkett-Smith Speech: "The War on (Black) Men through the Degradation of (Black) Women"

(she didn't say 'Black' but I'm sure that's what she meant)

"How is man to recognize his full Self, his full power through the eyes of an incomplete woman?
The woman who has been stripped of Goddess recognition and diminished to a big ass and full breast for physical comfort only.

The woman who has been silenced so she may forget her spiritual essence because her words stir too much thought outside of the pleasure space.
The woman who has been diminished to covering all that rots inside of her with weaves and red bottom shoes.

I am sure the men, who restructured our societies from cultures that honored woman, had no idea of the outcome.
They had no idea that eventually, even men would render themselves empty and longing for meaning, depth and connection.

There is a deep sadness when I witness a man that can't recognize the emptiness he feels when he objectifies himself as a bank and truly believes he can buy love with things and status. It is painful to witness the betrayal when a woman takes him up on that offer.

He doesn't recognize that the [creation] of a half woman has contributed to his repressed anger and frustration of feeling he is not enough. He then may love no woman or keep many half women as his prize.

He doesn't recognize that it's his submersion in the imbalanced warrior culture, where violence is the means of getting respect and power, as the reason he can break the face of the woman who bore him four children.

When woman is lost, so is man. The truth is, woman is the window to a man's heart and a man's heart is the gateway to his soul.

Power and control will NEVER outweigh love.

May we all find our way" ~ ***Jada Pinkett-Smith***

"AS BLACK MEN we cannot BITCH about the condition of our women if we are not PROTECTING our women, RAISING our daughters, or HONORING our mothers. We are the WARRIORS, and at some point we must realize that we have failed our black women to a certain extent in regards of HONOR and PROTECTION. We must begin again to FIGHT for HER and her HONOR; let's build for HER and HER/OUR CHILDREN; Let's take HER back as our QUEEN and PROVIDE a SECURE environment for HER to BE all that the POWER of her FEMI-NINE energy destined her to be, so that SHE can walk in HER DIVINE role in giving LIFE and NOURISHMENT to our CHILDREN, our FUTURE".

HOTEP, POWER, & RAspect Your brother/warrior ~ *Tau RA*

Now I'm fully aware that not all of us are descendants of the enslaved, and it's important to recognise that. For instance, if one person in the relationship is the descendant of an enslaved African and the other isn't, there could be issues around that. One person may not be able to relate to why the other person reacts the way they do. So whether you are or you aren't, it's still important to know how our *past* still affects us *today*, because it's still affecting our relationships with each other and our community as a whole. In fact, even those who were *not* sold into slavery were still affected by the slave trade; their families would have been ripped apart. Their leaders would have been killed. Their communities would not have been the same. Besides, those who weren't sold into slavery were still affected by *Colonialism*. I feel sad when I see indigenous Africans wearing European clothing instead of their own bright coloured African clothing made of natural cotton. Or a weave instead of their own natural braided hair. Or trying to make themselves look anything *but* African. It bothers me when I see a native African who still has their mother tongue but bleaches their skin. The psychological programming which causes them to do these things is so deep-rooted, that it's going to take a lot of work to *undo* the programming.

Work on Your Self First

Before we as Black women and men can begin to join ourselves to each other we have to work on *ourselves* first. You are not looking for someone to 'complete' you; both individuals should come into the relationship as two *whole* people, not two halves trying to make a whole.

"A life partner does not complete you; a life partner is icing on the cake of your own complete life. Do not look outside yourself for happiness. Then the relationship you truly want and need will come" ~ Eye'm King

Affirmation: *"I am whole and complete in my Self"*

You may have your list of all the qualities you want your 'dream man' to have, but when he comes along, will YOU be the type of woman that HE is looking for?

A Strong Black Man will be looking for a Strong Black Woman.

> The strongest actions for a woman is to love herself, be herself and shine amongst those who never believed she could.
> ~Author Unknown

Love Your Self!

Be Your Self!

Shine Amongst Those Who Didn't Believe in You!

And don't compromise Who You Are in order to please others.

Taken from **Year Four** of *'Single, Spiritual…AND Sexual!'* (The Goddess Theory):

- ♥ It is not true that I am nothing without a man in my life. The purpose of our relationship would not be for him to complete me, but for *me* to share my completeness with *him*!

- ♥ I love my Self: I do not seek love for my Self through another.

- ♥ My goal in life is to know the highest part of my Self, and to stay centred in that. (Blessed are the Self-centred, for they shall know God).

- ♥ My most important relationship therefore, must be with my *Self*. I must first learn to honour and cherish and love my Self. I must first see my *Self* as worthy, before I see another as worthy. I must first see my *Self* as blessed, before I see another as blessed. I must first know my *Self* as holy before I acknowledge holiness in another.

- ♥ I am becoming consciously aware of Who I Am (God in the flesh). My personal relationships are the most important element in this process. Therefore they are *holy ground*.

- ♥ I see all those I am in relationship with as sacred souls on a sacred journey. I will always strive to see the god/goddess in every body, even when they are showing me less.

- ♥ In relationship, I will only ever be concerned about my *Self*; not about the other. It doesn't matter what the other is being, doing, having, saying, wanting or demanding. It doesn't matter what the other is thinking or planning. It only matters what I AM BEING IN RELATIONSHIP TO THAT.

- ♥ What am I being? What am I doing? What am I having?

♥ My grandest dream, my highest idea, and my fondest hope should have nothing to do with my beloved *other*, but my beloved SELF.

♥ It's not how well my beloved other lives up to my ideas, or how well I live up to their ideas, but *how well I live up to my OWN ideas*.

♥ I will not lose my Self in my relationship. I will not give up Who I Am in order to be, or stay in a relationship.

♥ I am being the most loving person, because I am Self-centred.

♥ I am now and forever centred upon my SELF!

While you are single, use this time to develop your Self; start a Self-development programme. When I was a blocked writer and artist the book that helped me unblock after 20 years was *'The Artist's Way'* by Julia Cameron. It was a 12-week programme that involved *daily* and *weekly* exercises. Decide what part of your Self you wish to develop and find a course that will help you. It doesn't have to be one you have to go *out* to do, it can be one you do from home. Another book I would highly recommend is *'Heal Thyself'* by Queen Afua, which I have referenced in my Self-help novel *'Single, Spiritual…AND Sexual!'* That is another great book that assisted me on my Self-healing journey.

Learn how to meditate; this is another thing which really helped me deal with my negative thinking patterns (which is an on-going process).

"There are different levels of development; we believe that because we've got a grown body, that makes us a woman or a man; that's just a growth, but the development doesn't stop because your body's grown. It's inward. It's about spiritual maturity: spiritual, mental and emotional as well as the physical. And it's about developing all those levels of your Self. So what I'm saying is that the issues and the problems that we have is based on the erroneous way we relate to ourselves as male or female, and therefore how we relate to each other. So when this Willie Lynch thing was done upon us we have to look into the words 'Willie

Lynch' – our WILL has been LYNCHED. Your will to be what you want to be has been lynched, and you've been made into what someone else wants you to be. So you don't have your will to be yourself. You're being what someone else wants you to be. It's the WILL of the 'I' that can be what it wills to be. 'I' is the spiritual identity, not the physical idea or ego personality in which you're only thinking about yourself. No, we're dealing with your Self. What's good for you must be good for the Whole. See? It's that individual connection to the Whole, the Universal. And that is the true relationship to start with, to know. Our relationships are bringing us back to that fundamental principle of ourselves, for us to know what Love is, because even the way we think about Love is not Love, it's about desperation, it's about "Oh God, please send someone to fill up my emptiness". That's not Love, that's neediness, it's a fear of being alone, and these things have been played out through the media, through films, to be called 'Love'"
~ **Siayoum Atum Ab Ankh Rhem**

(In my poem *"I Am What I WILL to Be!"* I explain how I am using Positive Affirmations to *'change everything about me, re-creating Who I Am and Who I Wish to Be'*, and how you can too!)

You Are Not a Victim!

He did nothing to you that you didn't allow him to do! When you learn to Love and Respect your Self you will *command* Love and Respect from others – don't expect others to have for you what you don't have for your Self.

I have never and would never mess around with a married man. Women who sleep with other women's husbands thinking that they're going to leave their wife for them are only fooling themselves. On top of that, they are sowing bad seeds. If a married man will cheat on and leave his wife for you, what makes you think he won't do the same to you? Leave him alone!

Believe it or not, men are looking for a woman with *substance* to settle down with. Don't get me wrong, they *love* the booty-call woman, who they can have for sex with no real commitment other than to make sure they arrive before 10pm. And they love the woman they can parade at events like one of their boy toys. But what they are *really* looking for is a woman that they would be happy to introduce to their mother.

If you jump straight into bed with him, what would make him think you wouldn't do the same with any other man? Are you wife material?

I learnt that bitter lesson back in 2006. 'H' wasn't *married*, but he was in a relationship. I guess I felt justified because we had this on-off thing going since 2001. But it still hurt when he told me that he wasn't going to leave his girlfriend for me. I was so vex I wrote the poem *'Sex with the EX'* to give my sisters some stern advice about sleeping with their ex's. (He called me up about 6 weeks later to tell me that he *had* split up with her but the damage had already been done, and the poem had already been written).

Needless to say, we carried on our on-off relationship for another 6 years. He was the only brother I kept jumping in and out of a relationship (bed) with, based on the fact that we had this 'strong connection'. When we had our last 'encounter,' I just wanted to see if there was anything left. There wasn't. The relationship had well and truly died. We were in two very different places mentally. So the way my novel ended was symbolic of the end of our relationship. But have no fear! If you thought Charles was the best thing since sliced bread, wait 'til you read the sequel!

Do you insist on carrying on sleeping with a man even though you know there's nothing left there? Why do you do that to your Self?

"But I love him!" I hear you say.

Do you love him more than you love your Self? Put your Self first! If the relationship isn't serving you anymore, end it. Relationships aren't about what you can get out of them, but if you're giving, giving, giving and not getting anything back in return you're not doing any justice to your Self.

(When I say 'not getting anything back' I'm not referring to material things, in fact I will rarely be referring to material things).

Another thing, don't you think it's funny how Black brothers who have a white wife at home will still come to you looking for sex?

At the launch of a recent BHM exhibition I was taking part in, one of the artists came with his white wife. She came up to me and told me how much she admired my artwork and how distinctive it was, and how she was trying to help her husband (pointing him out) get his artwork 'out there'.

Later that same day, he came over and started chatting me up. I asked him if that wasn't his wife over there, to which he replied "Yes, but I'm a naughty boy". Later that evening, he proceeded to chat up another one of my sister-friends under the influence of the beer he was drinking. When I asked him why he had married a white woman since he clearly liked Black sisters, his lame excuse was "she was the strongest one at the time".

Now which white woman do you know who is stronger than a Black woman?

But they DO know how to get the ring on their finger.

One of my girlfriends had the same experience recently; we had attended a social evening for Black professionals and were encouraged to take each other's contact details.

My friend met up with one of the brothers a few days later, and it turned out he was married to a white woman, but was suggesting that he book a hotel room for them to share that night. When she asked him why he is still with his wife he replied "she would commit suicide if I left". Who's he trying to fool?

Are you still carrying Emotional Baggage from previous relationships?

'.....Each time I'm reminded of a negative experience it starts a chain reaction

I lash out, shout and scream, say words I don't mean

And before I know it, I'm alone again!'

*('**Love Attraction**' on the 'Seeds of Love' CD)*

Does this sound familiar? Do you find yourself reacting in a way you didn't intend to, based upon something that happened in a *previous* relationship? If so, you're still carrying Emotional Baggage! I wrote the poemsong *'Love Attraction'* just for you! The poem (guided by my inner voice) gives a step by step process for preparing your Self to meet your Soul Mate. All emotional baggage from previous relationships has got to be dropped. Then you need to work on your Self. Finally, you need to focus on the type of man you want to attract. When you feel ready for him, he'll show up.

Here's some advice from relationships expert **Nigel Beckles**:

"Have you worked on your personal development? Have you worked through any emotional baggage that may be sabotaging your relationship choices? Many men and women enter relationships with unresolved issues; unfortunately these issues eventually surface during the relationship causing unnecessary pain and drama. When you are single make time to work on yourself so you are the best version of yourself you can be.

Remember, a relationship is meant to enhance your life not be your life. Make sure you have your own plans, goals and dreams that do not include a man".

Taken from his book *'How to Avoid Making The BIG Relationships Mistakes!'* due for publication early 2014

What are you doing while you're waiting for your man to appear? Are you spending every evening watching 'programmes' on the tell-lie-vision? Or do you spend them on the phone, or Social Networking? Prepare yourself by *becoming* the type of person you wish to attract.

You Attract Who You Are

"There are some simple laws in the universe that we should remember, one being; good women attract good men, bad women attract bad men. In other words, we attract what we are. Women should not seek a man for money and sex or to see what material things she can get from him. Men find this behaviour off-putting, and eventually leave their women who behave like this, because

men find this type of woman to be very draining and leechy. If a woman has good intentions for a man he will see this through her behaviour towards him. If a woman can help a man with his life and his goals, he is more likely to put a ring on her finger, rather than one who just wants to leech him for his wealth and money, and also make his life a misery with her flirting, moaning and gold-digging" ~ **Yeshuah the 1st**, Conscious Hip-Hop Rapper

"I really don't consider any man or woman to be good or bad... I feel that we attract who we are and if a person can become that person he/she wishes to have a relationship with then they can attract that person to themselves....The primary reason for most relationships is so a person can work on their spiritual Self and karma! So with that said, the more you clear up issues for yourself, the more you ARE the 'right' person; the more you will attract the person you are looking for. Become that person who you desire and learn to love and understand Self first before you embark on a love quest." ~ **Wilfred 'Rawventure' Campbell**

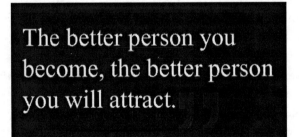

The better person you become, the better person you will attract.

"Exude love and send it out into the world. How others treat us is their path and how we react is ours...we are what we give" ~
Wilfred 'Rawventure' Campbell

Whatever you desire to attract in a man, develop it in your *Self*. Do you want a man who is loving? Be loving! Do you want a man who will respect you? Respect your Self! Do you want a man who is a good communicator? Be one yourself. Do you want a man who is spiritual? Then get in touch with your own spirituality.

'Self Love' by Cezanne

*"It's about being the type of person you want to see in someone else" ~ **Suraj Odekunle**, Seeds of Elevation*

My painting *'Self Love'* is symbolic: Our **thoughts are the seeds** and our **mind is the garden.** Thoughts rooted in Love produce a harvest of beautiful flowers, while thoughts rooted in fear produce weed-like thoughts (and you know how fast weeds grow, don't you?). Start cultivating your mind by learning how to uproot negative thoughts and replacing them with positive thoughts. When you are thinking *positive thoughts*, you radiate *positive energy*, when you are thinking negatively, you radiate negative energy. Depending on what frequency you are on, will determine what you attract to your Self (explained fully in my poem *'Fertile Soil'* on the *Seeds of Love* CD and in **Year Three** of my novel). The sun in the painting represents our Solar Plexus, where we as women *feel* from.

Orman Griffith is a very prolific and deep brother who I met on FB (who happens to like writing in CAPITALS). Take heed to his advice:

"It is said that "IT IS WONDERFUL TO BE ALONE ....AND REALLY FANTASTIC TO MEET YOUR REFLECTION"

The "GOOD BLACK MAN" DESERVES "A GOOD & GREAT BLACK WOMAN".

If this statement is true, each seeker must by definition be emboldened by the FULL REALIZATION of their WORTH & POTENTIAL.

Any relationship that is envisioned as productive & progressive with the ultimate aim of consummation in the UNION OF MARRIAGE must be tempered & forged in the un-quenching fires of the human disjoin of "The Lust of Power & The Power of Lust"

The contest to promote and provoke union has as its base several layers of complex and perhaps not often similar core structures of attraction and attractiveness, that weave into each other and embrace each other like strands of DNA that seek fusion at points that allow such union; and these points of cohesion may be as different as the poles of a magnet which when reversed can REPEL WITH THE SAME FORCE AS THEY ATTRACT.

Is this core of the attraction FEMININE BEAUTY & MALE MASCULINITY? Or is it RAW SEXUALITY LAYERED AS A HONEY TRAP?

Is it perhaps SOCIAL DEPENDENCY masked with FINANCIAL OPPORTUNITY because of PARENTING RESPONSIBILITY??

OR could it be RELIGIOUS NECESSITY MASQUERADING AS PURITAN?? SPIRITUALITY EVOLVING FROM DOGMA IMPRINTING???

The pressures that promote such a strong & perhaps DESPERATE DESIRE FOR UNION must be first TOTALLY UNDERSTOOD WITH HONESTY & CLARITY if either party is to avoid becoming another statistic of MARRIAGE MELTDOWN.

The WOMAN WITHIN THE WOMAN MUST FULLY RECOGNIZE THE MAN WITHIN THE MAN, and after each having carefully examined the 'BALANCE SHEET OF THE

OTHER', they must take the REINFORCED BUT CAREFULLY CALCULATED RISK to be EMBOLDENED BY THE POSSIBILITY OF A GREAT & GOOD OUTCOME OF SUCH A UNION.

There is no man who if and when presented with a GOOD & GREAT PROPOSITION will be stupid/foolish enough to turn it down when his TRUE SENSIBILITIES TELLS HIM HE IS A "JACKPOT WINNER"

The man who was once a prolific emotional encounter prospector, ONCE HE HAS FOUND THE PEARL OF GREAT PRICE or THE DIAMOND OF EXQUISITE EXCELLENCE WILL NEVER BE HESITANT IN CONFIRMING HIS DISCOVERY WITH ENTHUSIASM OF ACQUISITIVE POSSESSION

To the BEAUTIFUL SISTER IN WAITING TO BE CROWNED WOMAN & BRIDE OF THE BEDCHAMBER OF MARRIAGE UNION, I SAY..."INDEED YOU CAN TAKE THE HORSE TO THE WATER BUT YOU CANNOT MAKE IT DRINK" Hmmmmmmmm However your task is not to take the horse to the water at all........!!! YOUR TASK IS TO RUN THAT HORSE AROUND IN THE DELIGHT OF SKILLFUL EXERCISES THAT TONES & HONES ITS FITNESS FOR PURPOSE, THUS MAKING IT DRAMATICALLY THIRSTY......... A THIRSTY HORSE WILL & MUST DRINK" (smile)

DO YOU NOT KNOW THE CHARMS & THE ARTS OF A NUBIAN QUEEN???......DO YOU NOT ALSO KNOW THE DESIRES & WEAKNESSES OF YOUR NUBIAN KING???

HAS HE NOT SHOWN THESE THINGS TO YOU OFTEN ENOUGH!!! OR WERE YOU TOO BLINDED BY YOUR QUEST THAT YOU FAILED TO SEE HIS DYNAMIC & DRAMATIC MESSAGES?

HAS HE NOT OFTEN BECOME LIKE PLAY MOLD IN YOUR ARMS AS HE SUCCUMBED TO YOUR WONDERFUL CHARMS, AS OFTEN AS HE WITHOUT RESISTANCE TREATED YOU LIKE A QUEEN & UPHELD YOU WITH DIGNITY AS HIS QUEEN BECAUSE THIS WAS & IS HIS PURPOSE??

Hmmmmmmmmmmm Why then do you continue to PROCRASTINATE & TEMPT FATE WHEN THE FORTUNES OF LOVE HAS PRESENTED YOU WITH THE PRIZE OF LOVE!!!......A MAN WILLING TO BE CONQUERED.

NONE SO BLIND AS THOSE WHO THROUGH ANXIETY WILL NOT SEE.

EMBRACE YOUR REFLECTION!" ~ **Orman Griffith**

I love that; EMBRACE YOUR REFLECTION! He's right, sometimes we as women are so desperate to jump into bed with a man hoping that our bedroom antics will make him want to be with us forever, yet listen to what the men are saying themselves – make them wait!!!

The longer you make them wait, the more respect they seem to develop for you. Isn't that funny? Reminds me of the film *'Think Like a Man'*....

I think part of our problem as Black Women is we've forgotten Who We Are and the power that we have.

Know Your Power!

"The woman's energy is being manipulated because what a woman focuses on, she CREATES. That's why they give women all these soap operas with all these distressed emotions, and they're really getting into the feeling and the emotion and the hatred towards the male playing out various roles. Because **the womban gives form to creational ideas**, she's the one who is being manipulated to create all the craziness that is going on in the world" ~ *Siayoum Atum Ab Ankh Rhem*, Astrologer

I intuitively stopped watching tell-lie-vision over 10 years ago, because I was aware of the negative impact it was having on my emotions, especially the *news* (check to see how you *feel* after watching the news). At the time I stopped watching 'programs' I was beginning to learn about the creative power of my thoughts. I made it my duty to do my best to keep my Self feeling positive, in order to begin attracting positive things into my life. I also stopped listening to songs that made me feel dreary. It's amazing how many songs there are like that!

What type of man do you wish to attract? If you wish to attract a man who's positive, fun-loving, generous, kind-natured, spiritual, attractive, with an abundance mentality, develop it in your Self first – you have the power to *attract* that which you are! Have you heard of the Law of Attraction? Well in every polarity there's always its opposite; the opposite of the Law of Attraction is the Law of Repelling – what you're not *attracting*, you're *repelling*!

"When women walk the street and they're not in that open channel energy where they're flowing like water, where their orgasmic energy becomes this auric field around them of high vibration; when she's in that energy field she elevates the men she passes like "WOW!" If a woman smiles at a guy in the street she needn't worry that he's going to follow her home. No, the guy's just like "flippin' heck, you've just made my day!" You understand what I mean? Rather than having this war going on inside the auric field, the misery pulling you in an emotional dumpster and chucking it out at the men as they walk by. The men feel it, and when women turn around and become very insensitive to their own feelings, they're actually blocking out the sensitivity to realise that men FEEL. The man seeks to feel a woman's heart, to know what he's dealing with. While she's there in her head and closed to her heart, her man can tell" ~ **Siayoum Atum Ab Ankh Rhem**, Astrologer

Trust Your In-tuition

"The feminine energy was considered weak, because its intuitive power wasn't appreciated. We were all taught to THINK, not FEEL" ~ **Eye'm King**

Our strongest asset as women is our *intuition*. We are ruled by our *emotions*. We have an inner guidance system, which we are more in tune with than men are. Not to say that men don't have it as well, but ours is stronger. Men are more logical; they *think*, we *feel*.

What is intuition? Let's look at how I broke down the word: **In-tuition**, in other words, it's your **inner teacher** and guide. How many times have you heard that still, small voice within tell you to do something and you ignored it, only to exasperatingly say later "If only I had listened to my spirit!" So your in-tuition is there to *guide* you. You can feel it in your Solar Plexus, located at the back of your stomach. When you're on the right track you get a good feeling in your gut. When you're on the wrong track you get that churning feeling, warning you that you're going wrong. Learn to be guided by that.

*"What makes a womban different from a man is that Feminine Energy predominates; That's the intuition, the unconscious, the irrational (that which knows without knowing how it knows). The Black Woman represents the Primordial Cosmic Womb that works out the plans of Creation. Feminine energy is not limited to a physical body; although male and female have Feminine Energy, but if you're in a feminine body you must be in a predominantly Feminine Energy – not that the woman doesn't have the masculine, but the Feminine is your strong power point. And a man, his masculine is his strong power point. (Not that he doesn't have a heart that opens up, because that's the developing of the feminine in himself). So when we talk about Feminine Energy, we're talking about the expression of Consciousness Intelligence, learning from within, being able to tap in directly to the Universal Source. Intellect is an expression of intelligence, but intuition, which is FEELING is also an expression of intelligence. So the Feminine Energy is talking about your Emotional Intelligence. Feelings are conscious and intelligent, they are not wayward in irrational nonsense. A lot of us aren't emotionally intelligent at all. Emotional Intelligence allows us to **perceive without words through feeling vibrations**, knowledge, wisdom, insight, clarity, overstanding, comprehension, through the energy, the emotions, the FEELING aspect of you....so the Feminine Energy is about bringing balance and harmony to the intellect. You work together to create harmony and balance. Harmony is what is felt inside of us as Love, because Love is the inter-connectedness everything has with each other"* ~ **Siayoum Atum Ab Ankh Rhem**, Astrologer

Learn to TRUST YOUR IN-TUITION. Listen to what your inner guide is telling you to do, and follow it as often as possible. Sometimes the things it tells you to do may seem irrational. Once I was at a Business Seminar and one of the speakers was about to give away one of his packages worth thousands of pounds, which would have really helped to take my business to the next level. He told everyone to stand on their chairs. My inner voice advised me to stay standing on my chair, raise my hand in the air and shout "I WANT THE PACKAGE!" When he told everyone to get off their chairs and sit down again, I was too embarrassed to do what my inner voice had advised, and sat down with everyone else. The man picked out a random person from the audience and gave away the package. I was kicking myself for weeks after (still am now actually).

Even where relationships are concerned, you *feel* when something is right or wrong. Get in touch with your inner feelings, they are your guide. Remember, women go more by our *feelings*, men by their logic. The two are really meant to *compliment* each other. If both the man and woman operated in a logical manner, the relationship would lack feeling, and visa versa. As the woman, you must be in touch with the *feeling* part of your Self, which is your femininity.

Get in Touch with Your Femininity

"The Black Woman represents the Primordial Womban. Therefore, she's supposed to be the most feminine. She's supposed to be the most balanced being, which means that she is FEMININE, and that she respects and embraces the MASCULINE. She loves the masculine because it is part of her. When a woman is in a physical, feminine body she has to be in tune to the integrity of the vehicle, because that's what the soul has chosen to incarnate in (same with a man). So therefore there's a role a woman plays when we're talking about a woman in a feminine vehicle that can give birth. She's got to innerstand her creative power and how that is used so she can bring balance to the planet" ~ **Siayoum Atum Ab Ankh Rhem**, Astrologer

What does being feminine mean to you? We as Black women must give up the Eurocentric idea of what being feminine is and get back to our own cultural ways of dealing with our men, in order for our relationships to work.

"Where do women get their ideas of what being feminine is? Consumerism: You're inadequate if you don't wear lipstick, or Chanel perfume, or if you don't buy this dress or move like these women, or have that type of body. So women aren't even paying attention and tuning into their own femininity, they're just trying to compete with each other. The idea of femininity these days has been distorted, more so than in the days when we were growing up, because we knew our gender...Then around the middle of the 80's they started designing unisex clothing, so now women could dress in men's clothes. They didn't say men could dress in women's clothes, check that out, they made clothes for women to dress and look like men, and the women are thinking this means equality". ~ **Siayoum**

More recently, they have begun dressing up *men* in *women's* clothes! Can you see how the male and female energies are being distorted?

As part of preparing your Self to meet your soul mate, find out as much as you can about the Afrocentric way of being a woman as possible. The book *'An Afrocentric Guide to a Spiritual Union'* by Ra Un Nefer Amen is a good place to start. This book inspired parts of my poem *'R U The One?'* (featured in the poetry section of this book)

"Firstly, a woman needs to be in her feminine energy/ femininity otherwise the man has nothing to interact with, unless he's interacting with another man. There's a difference in THINKING you're feminine and FEELING feminine. It's about the right relationship between Male and Female. There has to be MUTUAL HONOUR. There has to be MUTUAL RESPECT. You cannot respect the Divine Feminine while you trash the Divine Masculine; "The Creator is not Male, it's Female!" Let's not move to these extremes and think we're progressing here! Feminine receives the masculine. Without the Feminine receiving

44

*the masculine there's nothing for them to give form to or express. Truth is reflected even in your anatomy; the eggs are just sitting there; it's the sperm that has to come along and activate the woman to release the potential of what's being held there. People talk about the moonlight, but the moon only reflects the light of the sun. In nature, the moon goes around the sun, it reflects the sun's light. The woman is the **moon**, and the man is the **sun**.*

'My King' by Cezanne

(The Adinkra symbol represents the Sun and the Moon)

The woman's role is to reflect the light of the sun. If the moon didn't reflect back the light of the sun, the sun wouldn't know what its purpose was for. So when the man projects his light, a woman should be able to take in that light, and reflect that light back to him so that he can feel himself; he knows himself because she has reflected him back to himself in all his glory, no holds barred. Then he feels strong, he feels his power, and then she makes herself more receptive for him to get closer to her. She is to receive and reflect back, not hold on to that energy and not reflect it back to him.

A woman shouldn't use her sexuality to manipulate the man's energy, she should use it to uplift, nourish, heal and restore confidence in the man, so he can be himself. She gives him drive, he gives her direction. So if a woman's not respecting the masculine because she's been conditioned to believe that being a woman is about LOOKING like one but not FEELING like one and OPERATING like one; she wants to contest and challenge the male, and that makes the man either have to let go of his masculinity and become effeminized, then what ends up happening is he rebels out of not feeling like a man. Because we've been conditioned from this Willie Lynch thing to switch the roles and then the whole of society and the whole world based on a Western interpretation of Male and Female e.g. men are from Mars and Women are from Venus, making people think that the natural relationship between Male and Female is alienation between each other. That's not the nature of it, that the UN-natural nature of it! You cannot have a harmonious relationship if you're not in the right gender energy to have that compatibleness, because the man will have no woman to interact with, he's interacting with another male! Or she attracts to herself a man who's more in touch with his feminine energy, rather than his masculine energy. When I say 'behind every good man is a powerful woman' I'm not talking in the physical sense (although that can be the case), it's about a man who has a strong, cultivated, developed feminine force behind him, so he feels that the feminine force fortifies his masculinity. But we have a society that tells women that men are a load of this or that, or that men are suppressing women, and then the women believe to themselves that their femininity is a weakness and that they need to be like the men.

If a man is giving and the woman is receiving but she's not reflecting back then it becomes an imbalanced energy. A man will hold back if he's not being received like a man. If a woman is not being feminine in her energy e.g. she's being challenging, controlling, on a male polarity it's not healthy for her. A woman needs to stop believing her feminine energy is weak, and to surrender" ~ **Siayoum Atum Ab Ankh Rhem**, Astrologer

I asked Saiyoum: How should a woman be in her feminine energy? *"Be open, be gentle, be soft. There's no weakness in that. A lot of women are very hard. You see the body's an emotional filter, so whatever your thoughts and feelings are will reflect through the physical form".*

The Strength of a Woman Can Become Her Biggest Flaw
by Darren Moxam

"Throughout the ages it has always been biblical law that the man provides and the woman is the lady of the house. She looks after the nest, cooks, cleans whilst the man brings the fruits home. However through generations a woman's independence has come to the forefront and as the woman becomes more independent the man becomes less depended on. This is not a bad thing however as long as balance in the relationship remains. Men have egos and pride, and a man's manhood is easily disrupted if he is not able to show his worth. He needs that ego boost as much as he needs to hear the words "You have done a good job."

It's like growing up, we tend to be very close to our mothers, even protective towards them and every time our mother says "Well done son," that's the encouragement we need in our conquest and journey towards becoming a man. We are being recognised for our manhood achievements, something we require from our spouse later on down the line.

What women have to realise is that it's not always about what they can do and what they are capable of but more so what they'll allow us men to take care of. Now when writing something like this I tread very carefully because one thing is for certain, a woman that can take care of business is the kind of woman any good man needs so I chose to use the word allow, showing I am not against a strong woman. We need a strong woman who will allow us that control and if we fail at any time, to have our back because the woman is the backbone of the relationship. This is not to say we as men should take advantage knowing you are there to pick up the pieces but more there as support of us, knowing we are trying. We are being men.

If a woman works, cooks, cleans, takes care of the kids and directs the path where the family are heading becoming overly self-reliant the balance in the relationship shifts and then you have to beg the question; what attributes is he the man bringing to the table? The truth is ladies we all know that many of you can cook, clean, take care of the kids, look after the house whilst doing DIY at the same time simultaneously if you put your mind to it but because you can doesn't mean you have to. Let a man take care of his man business. The man is called man for a reason. He is there to sweat, get dirty so allow him to be your Mandingo. Then afterwards tell him how much you love him and how much he has done a good job even if you could do it better" ~ copyright © 2013 **Darren Moxam**, Author/Poet/Writer

Are you hearing what the men are saying, ladies? You play *your* role as the woman in the relationship, and let him play *his*! So, in preparation for meeting your soul mate, your homework is to practice operating in your feminine energy as much as possible, and to find out as much about the Afrocentric way of being a woman as possible. If you're a man reading this book, your job is to operate in your masculine energy, and find out how you should operate in the relationship from an *Afrocentric* point of view. Some men just need to grow up!

Do you want to attract a MAN or a BOY?

"A lot of women want men to cater to their childishness, their selfishness, their little girl. They'll quickly turn around and say "I don't see no man, you're a boy!" but don't you see what you're doing? You're encouraging men to stay, or revert them into that boyish role. When he comes as a man you rebel against it because only one man can be in the house, and it has to have the skirt, or it must be you. What's going on with that? It's like when a mother, instead of encouraging her son to be confident in himself to be free and independent of her, she treats him like a little girl; "Oh, my little boy" No, no, no! In some cultures it is accepted that when the girl grows up she will leave home, marry, and go live with her husband. But they expect the boy child to stay at home for the rest of his life and look after his mother when she gets old, as if to say

48

that's her reward for giving birth to him. These types of things demasculate a man because it keeps him as a boy loved by the mother, not a man loved by a woman. And this has been intentionally done (by them), and perpetuated by ourselves.

What you have now is the psychology that takes the woman and tells her 'make your daughter like you'. She has to be independent. You can't rely on a man. So you make her strong and independent. Now the boy, anytime his masculinity comes up, you better put that fire out straight away because you can't be contending to be a man, because there's only one man (the white man). This is the Willie Lynch psychology. So the Black boy gets suppressed by his mother, because she's scared he's going to go out and get killed, so he is kept as a boy. In the 60's, a lot of what Black men were shouting out for was to be recognised as a MAN. Whereas the white man would just tell you "you're a boy". In Jamaica and other places, the elders want to refer to you as a boy. You see the psychology? So what happens now, a woman may end up what she thinks is loving a man is actually being a mother to a son. Some men will be looking for that. He may do everything around the house; it's not based upon the same expressions that was in the past; hunter, gatherer, provider. We (Black men) can't hunt and gather now because we're in a concrete jungle. We're in a totally different type of society. So the male principle is expressing itself in a different way. But the female principle must be in tune with herself to express herself, still feminine, but in a different way. So the principles of creation keep us in tune with what it is, but they're getting confused by taking on each other's roles like they're in competition and fighting each other. You've got a whole homosexual scenario, you've got a lot of lesbians, and you have a lot of bisexuality. So you're seeing a confusion and perversion with the sexual energy because it's not being embraced correctly" ~ **Siayoum Atum Ab Ankh Rhem**, Astrologer

From now on, your 'homework' will be to practice being feminine, and allowing the men in your life to be masculine (including your suns if you have boy children).

Once you have prepared your Self to meet your match, you will then be ready to start 'putting it out there'.

You Attract What You Think About Most

Do you focus on what you *want* in a man, or what you *don't want*? I wrote this poemsong (with the help of my Higher Self) to help YOU best prepare to meet and marry your soul mate:

Love Attraction

I've been on my own too long
And I'm tired of spending my nights alone
I'm looking for a love that's true
Someone to call my very own

Lord can you help me please
To attract the man of my dreams
Tell me what I have to do
To attract a love that's true?

Please...

Oh Lord, show me the way
To find the perfect One for me
What steps must I take to
bring the man from my dreams into reality?

(Inner Voice)
First I must heal my Self from the emotional damage
caused by past relationships
The hurt, the pain,
the wounds that keep opening up again and again
Each time I'm reminded of a negative experience
it starts a chain reaction;
I lash out, shout and scream, say words I don't mean
And before I know it, I'm alone again!

Please...

Oh Lord, show me the way
What steps do I have to take
To find the perfect One for me
Who'll give me the commitment that I seek?

(Inner Voice)
I must learn to drop the emotional baggage
I've been carrying around for years
Let go of all my insecurities and fears
Releasing bitterness, hurt and pain
Forgiving, so I can heal from within
And learn to love and trust again

And then, I must BE the Love I seek for my Self
I must love my Self unconditionally
And treat my Self how I'd like others to treat me
When I fill my Self up with Love,
I'll become a Love Magnet
Attracting that which I am

"I love you..."   *(look in the mirror and repeat to your Self)*

(Inner Voice)
Self Love has to come first
Because if I don't find love within, how can I accept if from him?
Besides, I cannot give what I haven't got,
So when I learn to love my Self in all my natural beauty
The person I meet will simply be a reflection of me!

Hmmm...

Next, I must focus on the things I desire in a man
Because if I keep focusing on the things I don't want,
I'll just keep attracting the same thing over and over again!
My desire is the beginning of creation
I'm attracting the man of my dreams
With my thoughts, words and actions
And I'm putting it out there with deep-felt gratitude
"Thank You!"

Now I feel ready for him...

I believe in a Love so true
But I know I've got work to do

I know that when I'm ready
My True Love will come to me
I believe in a Love so real
Someone with whom I can feel
Open and unrestrained
And with him I can trust again

(Inner Voice)
And lastly, I must put action to my beliefs
*Without **action** there can be no att**raction***
(The Law of Attraction is the Law of Love in action)
So I must do something POSITIVE to cause the manifestation
Of this 'Love Thing' that I'm seeking
I must create a space for him to appear,
Clear out the clutter of past interactions
Cutting ties, saying goodbyes to the love distractions
Who can't commit because of their own fears...

Now I trust and let go because I know that
DREAMS DO COME TRUE.
© Cezanne 2010

What Are You 'Asking' For?

This brings us to the subject of PRAYER.

What messages are you sending 'out there' when you say you want a husband?

What are you praying for? *How* are you praying? Are you *speaking it into being*, or just begging? If you are 'praying' from a begging point of view e.g. "Oh Lord, please grant me this one wish; Give me a husband, I beg you...Thank you Lord"

Or "Dear Father in Heaven, you know I've been faithful to Your Word. I've not had sex before marriage and I've waited patiently for the last 18 years for you to provide me with a husband. I'm going to be 40 next week and I'm still not married. Dear Lord, I really would like to have a child before menopause lik me. Your Word says that you supply all my needs according to Your glorious riches in Christ Jesus, so whe' me husban' deh?"

Needless to say, this isn't 'praying'. I'm sure you've prayed these kind of prayers many times before in real sincerity, and still nothing's happened.

You 'pray' with your thoughts, words and actions. When you think a thought, that's the *first* level of creation. **Thoughts are energy**; they go out into the universe and stick together with other like-thoughts. For instance, if your predominant thoughts are of meeting and marrying your soul mate, and you have a number of things on your list of qualities you'd like him to have, and he is *also* putting thoughts out there about finding his soul mate, with qualities similar to yours, you are more likely to be attracted to each other.

When you **speak your thoughts**, that's the *second* level of creation. **Words are vibration.** Your *voice* commands your mind, body and spirit. The **actions** you put to your thoughts and words are the *third* level of creation; when your thoughts, words and actions are all in agreement, whatever it is you are thinking about, speaking about and putting action to will eventually become your reality. Are your thoughts, words and actions moving you closer towards your goal of meeting your Soul Mate, getting married and starting a family? When you speak with *emotion* it affects your body on a cellular level. Help your Self by speaking the Absolute Truth. Keep your thoughts, words, and actions *positive* (your feelings will naturally follow). Empower your Self by using these tools wisely! Repeat this Affirmation out loud 10 times a day:

"I am meeting and marrying my soul mate"

Can you feel your body vibrating?

That's the Law of Attraction in Action!

ENERGY + VIBRATION = MATTER...

Don't Believe the Hype!

Now let's move onto the topic of subliminal messaging in films/the media.

Have you seen the film *'A Good Man is Hard to Find'*?

If you look on the front cover of the DVD, there are three Black Women looking at a Black Man. The subliminal message is that a good BLACK man is hard to find.

Plot Summary and I quote: 'Amidst claims that the African-American family is slowly deteriorating, filmmaker Leslie Small sets out to explore how **the role of Black women in the family has evolved as the population of Black males continues to diminish.** Small's film follows three women as they battle temptation (the film has a religious overtone) and contend with their personal demons while waging a valiant battle to maintain happy, healthy relationships'.

Try Something New?

Then there's the film *'Something New'* where the Black woman chooses the white dude over the good Black man (Blair Underwood no less!)

Storyline: 'Kenya McQueen is a successful African-American CPA, working her way to the top of the corporate ladder -- but her life has become all work and no play. Urged on by her friends to try something new and to let go of her dream of the "ideal Black man," she accepts a blind date with an architectural landscaper named Brian, only to cut the date short upon first sight, because Brian is white. The two meet again at a party, and Kenya hires Brian to landscape her new home. Over time, they hit it off, but Kenya's reservations about the acceptance their romance will find among her friends and family threatens everything. An intelligent romantic comedy that chooses to deal with issues of race and perception in a straight-forward way, from a point of view not often seen: that of a successful, upper-class black woman. (They neglected to mention that there was also a 'good Black man' fighting for her attention).

Bodyguard?

And in the film *'The Bodyguard'* it's the white man who is the Black Woman's knight in shining armour. Even in the film *'Blood 'n Bone'* (which I particularly liked) the Black man saves the *white* woman while the Black woman is left wanting. What better bodyguard or saviour could a Black Woman possibly want or need than a strong Black Man?

Watch out for the subliminal messages placed in films!

Take *'Diary of a Mad Black Woman'* as another example. Here we have an affluent Black couple; she had helped him build his business over a number of years and supported him on his way to the top, then when he finally became successful, he kicked her out and moved his white mistress and their love-child in.

Then there's *'Why Did I Get Married?'* and *'Why Did I Get Married Too'*. Here we have three high earning professional Black couples, and none of them were having any sex! What's that all about? I can understand the couples facing marital problems, but in none of the two films did it show a loving sex scene (or anything close to it). Call me 'too romantic' or liking to see the world through rose-coloured glasses, but I would have thought that the point of these films would be to show that successful Black couples *can* have loving relationships! Instead, there was marital infidelity, estrangement, abuse, divorce, and bitter heartache. The only couple who were really holding it together were Jill Scott and her hubby (gorgeous!). Does marriage have to be like that? Are there any successful Black couples out there? (And by successful I don't just mean in their careers).

The film *'For Colored Girls'* had to be the worst of them all. One Black Woman was being beaten up badly by her husband (he eventually killed their two children), another was date-raped in her home...and to be honest I can't remember anything more about that film, I had to block it out. But what is the subliminal messaging regarding our Black Men in all these films? Where's the film that will portray our Black Men as fine examples of character, mental strength and dignity?

Even the film *'Coming to America'* had me thinking. When I first saw it all those years ago (before my third eye was opened) I thought it was great. They actually brought out a film with some rich African culture in it. But Prince Akim left his African Bride, a Good Black Woman (who they degraded by having her bark like a dog and appear docile) to go to America to pick up a 'smart' mix raced woman, and bring her back to Africa to take place on the throne with him as King. What was wrong with all the African women why he had to go to America and choose a queen who wasn't even fully Black? And while they were in America, instead of helping the poor Black community they were staying in, they donated their wealth to the two white tramps. Hmmm….

Nowadays, the imagery everywhere is pointing to Black Men being with white women, and Black Women being with white men. Are you going to believe that this is the way to go? Or are you going to believe that *'We Belong Together'*?

Are you allowing your Self to be 'programmed' by these messages? Do you believe that there is a lack of 'good Black men?' Are you thinking about 'trying something new?'

Actually, I *can* think of one film that portrayed the Black Man in a positive light; *'Are We There Yet?'* and its sequel *'Are We Done Yet?'* The Black Man (played by Ice Cube) gave up his playboy ways to be with a single mother with two children (played by Nia Long). The children really put him to the test, including wrecking his 'wheels'. The couple eventually get married and have a baby of their own, amidst all the trials and tribulations.

You See What You EXPECT To See

When you think about Black men, what is your perception? Do you think "All the good Black men are already married" or "Black men are either in prison, on drugs, or with white women" or "Most men my age have at least one child, why can't I meet a man who's childless, like me? I don't want all the baby mamma drama!" or do you think "There are plenty of Good Black Men out there who are still single and childless, and I'm going to find one!"

You can only see what you *perceive* to see.

I was talking to a girlfriend recently who was convinced that Caribbean men don't want marriage. She asked whether a Caribbean woman seeking marriage should avoid Caribbean men. I told her that out of all the friends I grew up with, I'm the only one who isn't married, and most of us are Caribbean. She had recently had a baby for her long-term partner who lives in the Caribbean. Because *he* didn't want marriage, she had somehow built up a perception that 'Caribbean men don't want marriage'.

I know lots of 'good Black men'. Some I've met in person, and some through Social Networking. Now I'm not saying FB is an ideal place to meet your Soul Mate, but a good proportion of the men who have contributed to this book are single and most of them are on FB. Some people say there are loads of weirdos on Facebook and while I'm not denying this, I happen to believe that you attract what you are. The type of men I attracted to contribute to this book are deep thinkers, like my Self; *there are loads of 'good Black men' looking for a good Black Woman*! Are you seeing them? If not, why not?

When a brother can speak as articulately as this, I know he's not just a 'Good Black Man', but a brother with his third eye wide open:

"Nobody was put on this earth to find God. You didn't know anything about a God until somebody came with a book and convinced you that there was one beyond the sky somewhere. Then they used a fear tactic by telling you that you were lost and if you don't find and believe in God you will die and burn in hell forever. So out of fear you converted to a religion and told everybody you know that you found God. But God is a concept created by man to soothe his conscience and to justify his culture and worldly endeavours whether good or bad, and religion was formulated by man to conquer and control people of the masses. Don't take my word for it, family. Check out history. The God concept and religion puts you in bondage with its rules, regulations, and rituals and keeps you from walking in the Divine nature that you were already born with, family. You don't need no damn religion. You are divine. You were already born with a moral compass to know right from wrong as you navigate through this life. You were already born with a moral code in your spirit. You call it your conscience. You were already born with the spiritual ability to connect with the moral arc of the universe. You don't need to find God. In fact you already have met God. When they pulled you out of the womb they cut your umbilical cord and put you in the arms of God, your MaMa. My black MaMa is the first God I know.

I know my religious brothers and sisters gone think this is blasphemous, but I respect y'all beliefs. What I wrote above is what I know.

Peace and Prosperity, family" ~ **Tau RA** (posted on his FB status)

Are You Ready?

Relationships are hard work, are you sure you're ready for this? Are you ready to put in the WORK? It's one thing to get *into* a relationship, *sustaining* it is another. No matter how specific you are about the man you want to attract and he shows up exactly as you 'asked', there's still going to be work to do. After all, this is a merging of two souls, *physically*, *mentally* and *spiritually*.

The Law of Attraction is a powerful force in the universe. When I first found out about it in 2008, I decided to have fun with it and 'ordered' a dark Piscean brother with locs. The first one who turned up was a great guy, a great communicator, but the chemistry just wasn't there. The second one showed me the Certificate of Incorporation for his company on the day we met, so although he was broke and sleeping on a friend's couch, I thought at least he had *potential*. I was willing to work with that and do whatever I could to help him reach his goals. I invited him to bring his computer equipment to my house so he could have unlimited access to the internet (his excuse for not being able to make progress on his business was lack of internet usage to be able to set up his website). However once his computer was set up, he seemed to enjoy spending most of his time on Facebook chatting cowpat with his friends. I watched him operate for about 3 weeks before asking him to leave.

Be Specific!

'Know What You Want' by **Nigel Beckles**

'What type of man are you looking for? What type of qualities are you looking for in a partner? People make lists before going shopping for one simple reason; they want to come home with all the items they want or need! The bottom line is if you don't know what type of man you are looking for you are unlikely to meet him. Be very clear about the qualities you expect in a partner and do not compromise on them or you may fall in the trap of trying to change him, setting the scene for potential conflict'.

© **Nigel Beckles**, Author of '*How to Avoid Making The BIG Relationships Mistakes!*' due for publication early 2014

"The notion that Black sisters dream of marrying a 'Good Black Man' in my opinion is a flawed concept. Firstly, it presupposes that most Black men are somehow bad... and secondly, that most sisters just want to marry and settle down into some blissful Happy Ever After Being Single syndrome. The truth is what sisters want are similar to what most other ethnic groups of women want. That is a partner who will be faithful, as well as be able to protect and provide. By the latter I mean adding to the pot as most sisters nowadays can happily provide for themselves. The problem - if there is one - is one of compatibility. i.e. A sister might meet a brother that ticks all of the above boxes, but may not be the best looking brother, or may even be seen as boring if he doesn't have a bit of an edge. Likewise, a brotha may not be attracted to certain sisters if their hair is not in a particular style, or they don't have a particular figure size, or skin shade, etc. Everyone has a criteria - some will decide compatibility based on race (or race difference), religion, culture, profession even sex. Truth is, a person whether male or female, have to decide what is best for them and try not to compromise too much. What works for one sister may not for another. As the saying goes - it's different strokes for different folks" ~ ***Jak Beula*** (Creator of the game 'Nubian Jak')

I can relate to that statement. When I met 'H' in 2001 I had relaxed hair, a weave, loved dressing in high heels, make-up, the lot. Over the years I evolved and those things were no longer important to me. I transitioned from the wigs, weaves and straighteners to my natural hair. He didn't like my locs. Once he made a comment that he could just imagine me smoking a spliff. Even though the chemistry was still there, he didn't like the way I looked or dressed, and he couldn't help showing it on his face. When we first met he was overweight but I didn't pay any attention to it. In 2007 he lost all the weight, bought himself a brand new set of designer clothes and a Mercedes convertible. He started attracting 'model-type' women. He once made a comment that he likes 'girly-type' women when I couldn't be bothered to paint my nails for our date. So whereas Charles encouraged Suzanne to transition to her natural self in my Self-help novel, 'H' was the opposite. We actually had an argument once about weaves; he was *defending* women who wear them, while I was trying to explain the spiritual aspect of covering your crown chakra with somebody else's DNA (explained fully in **Year Three** of *'Single, Spiritual...AND Sexual!'*:'Think Kink'). When I told him that I was more focused on my 'inner Self' these days, he said that was just an excuse for my laziness in not bothering with my appearance. He was right to a certain extent; I don't have an hour a day to spend on my hair, make-up and nails. Ladies, if your man isn't going to support you going natural it's not your *hair* that has to go, it's the *man*.

If you're looking for a specific type of person, make sure that you're that type too, or you may not be compatible when you meet. If you're into the wigs and the weaves and the man you are trying to attract is into the natural look, it might not work (unless he's like the Charles character in my novel, who would be willing to help nurture you back to your naturalness!).

Ultimately, looks should *not* be the deciding factor in choosing a mate.

Be Realistic!

Do you have unrealistic expectations of what you're looking for in a man?

If a brother shows up and he's not working, or is in a low-paying job, would you consider him? Many of our men have high intellect, ambition and drive, but their potential has been held back by 'the system'. Would you consider one of them? If not, why not?

In my poem *"I Need a MAN!"* the Career Woman has the nice house, the flash car, all the money in the bank she needs etc. but no man. She is willing to take on a man who is earning less than herself, as long as he can make himself useful around the house (he must also have ambition to better himself!). I believe that in this day and age where there are more Black women in well-paid employment than Black men, it is important to make the effort to consider dating a Black Man who is earning less, and not make him feel inadequate in the process. Allow him to be the man.

And don't say "he has to be over 6ft" if you're 5ft nothing. Height should be proportional to your own height.

Don't go for looks alone, either. Of course there has to be a level of attraction, but be prepared to let love grow, instead of thinking it has to be love at first sight.

"Women need to learn to live within their means and stop putting unnecessary pressure on their man; some men get themselves into a lot of debt just to provide for his woman. She has set the bar at an unrealistic level. Her expectations are unrealistic. The same goes for men; men who watch a lot of pornography have unrealistic expectations in their sex life. If you are a ten-bolt battery, operate at your capacity; be realistic of what you are capable of. In the old days, people were content, they were happy just to have a partner. Nowadays, couples are busy on FB, BB, spending more time Social Networking than with their own partner. Be realistic and operate within the parameters of your own relationship. Stop looking into other people's gardens and tend to your own soil" ~ **Bunmi**

Rather than focus on what he's got, focus on the qualities he has.

Write the Vision, Make it Plain!

As I mentioned before, thoughts are one level of creation, words are another. The written word is powerful (check this book out for instance!).

Your goal is to get your *thoughts, words* (both spoken and written) and *actions* in line with each other.

So buy a journal (if you don't already have one).

Put the date.

You're going to make a list of all the things you wish to attract into your life.

Make sure the words you use move you closer towards your desires, not away from them!

In this society we've been taught to use language that *disempowers* us. For instance, sentences starting with "It's hard...", "I can't...", "I won't...", "I don't like...", "I don't believe...", "I haven't.... etc will literally stop growth, put a block in your way, and stop you from achieving. It is a *taught behaviour* that is *designed to hold you back.*

Words like "I'm trying...", "I can try...", "I'll try...", "I will attempt..." will cause you to try over and over again and never get anywhere. It is another *conditioned behaviour* designed to *hold you back.*

However words like "I am...", "I can...", "I will...", "I believe...", "I can do it...", "It is done...." Literally *promotes growth.* "I am" and "I can" is a command to your Self. It allows your wants, dreams and desires to come true. Using good words is a *learned behaviour.*

Start by drawing a line down the middle of your page. Write Positive Affirmations on the left side of your journal that will move you closer towards your goal of meeting and marrying your soul mate. Write your intentions in the Present Tense, as if they have already happened. Choose ones from below which resonate with you, but also feel free to make up your own:

"I am preparing my Self for my husband"

"I am getting to know my Self better and better"

"I am in perfect health; mind, spirit and body"

"I am whole, perfect and complete in my Self"

"I am so happy and grateful now that I am happily married to my soul mate"

"I am meeting and marrying my soul mate"

"I can FEEL him coming!"

"I can share my life"

"I can make a new beginning"

"I feel secure now that I am living in my own home with my husband"

"I am so happy now that I am loving mother"

"I can start a family"

"My life is changing drastically"

"I am ready for love"

Then on the right side of the page, next to each affirmation write how it makes you FEEL. Lastly GIVE THANKS that your wishes have been granted.

Feeling grateful and giving thanks BEFORE your 'dream man' shows up is an important part of the process. Get excited that he's on his way, and BE EXPECTANT!

Creative Visualisation Relaxation (I was going to say 'Exercise', but the point is to RELAX!)

Lie down on your bed or sofa. Close your eyes and allow yourself to relax completely. Starting with your head, concentrate on relaxing every muscle in your body; your face, neck, shoulders, arms, hands, fingers, hips, legs, feet and toes. If you have some meditation music, use this to help you relax. Once you are in a completely relaxed state, begin to imagine what your life would look like if you were *already* married to your Soul Mate. Build a clear picture in your mind in all its detail; *see* it, *feel* it, *taste* it, *touch* it, *smell* it. Imagine what it would *feel* like to be so completely in tune with your soul mate, someone who you can be totally open and free with, and who is totally open and free with you. Someone who compliments you, finishes your sentences (shows that you are on the same wavelength mentally), whom you can laugh, cry and be completely open with each other. Where would you be living? How many children would you have? What type of lifestyle would you be living? Feel the feelings of having it NOW!

When the idea for *'Love Bump'* popped into my mind, I wasn't thinking anything about its composition at all. I didn't think it up. I was simply relaxing on the sofa listening to a track by one of my favourite underground groups *Fertile Ground* called 'Fertile Ground', when the image just flashed into my mind in all its detail. Even though it was only for a split second it left an *impression*, and I was able to draw all the detail. It took me about 3 months to get around to painting it though, because I couldn't really relate to it. I'd already made my contribution to the world's population and it is not my desire to have any more babies, or to have the 'White Wedding'.

I asked my Higher Self what the painting meant, as there's always a symbolic meaning to them. The answer I received was that this painting is a tool to help YOU attract your soul mate; if it is your desire to meet your soul mate, get married and start a family you should focus on this image every day; if you're a woman, you would imagine that the woman in the painting is YOU, and if you are a man, that the man in the painting is YOU. Focus on the image every day for around 10-15 minutes in a relaxed state (ideally just before you go to sleep). Imagine what it would *feel* like to be in that position. This is the most important part; create the feelings inside as if you have *already* met your soul mate, got married, and are expecting your first child together. How would that make you *feel*? Get in touch with your *feelings*, feel it NOW! By the Law of Attraction, you will begin to magnetize yourself to your desire. The rest of the time you're not practising your Creative Visualisation, think and speak positively about your situation.

*"Know the difference between DREAMS and DESIRES. Live your dreams, not your desires. Rest, relax, sleep and meditate in order to have your **dreams** become clear to you, and not be overcome by your **desires**".* ~ **Vidal Montgomery**

In other words, don't get you DREAMS and DESIRES in a twist! If it's your *dream* to marry, keep your sexual *desires* under control!

I'm sure a lot of people assume from the title of my Self-help novel *'Single, Spiritual...AND Sexual!'* that I'm promoting promiscuity, but that's not the case at all; in the 11-year period that the story covers, the main character only had two lovers, one of which she married in the end. The book is more about getting in touch with your sexuality and spirituality, and knowing how the two are related. I have to admit, some of the sex scenes are quite graphic, but that's because my intention was to break the taboo around sex and spirituality. I also used the book to stretch my imagination to its limit (before realising it didn't have any!)

Coming from a Christian background, my sexuality had been suppressed. I wasn't supposed to *think* about sex let alone do it! And the more I wasn't supposed to think about or do it, the more I wanted to (and did). Since leaving the church, I've learnt the proper use of my sexual energy, and that my sexual energy is the same energy that I use to CREATE. I've learnt how to *transmute* my sexual energy rather than dissipate it (I hardly even masturbate anymore!). Our religious and educational institutions will never teach us what we really need to know where our *spirituality* and *sexuality* are concerned. They have severed the two, making us believe that sex and spirituality cannot be connected, when they are. Can you imagine what would happen if we were to remember Who We Are, and the power that we have when we (the Black Man and Black Woman) come together in a high state of consciousness?

This might be getting a bit too deep for this book – after all, we're still aiming to *get* together!

Prepare Yourself!

If you really believe he's on his way, get ready!

What are the majority of your thoughts around Love and Marriage? If you're thinking one thing and saying something else, you're not being congruent with your Self. For example, do you often think how nice it would be to come home to a man, to be married, or to be 'in love'? Then on the other hand you tell your girlfriends that you don't need a man, that you're happy for him to just come and 'service' you, or that you don't mind the fact that you're not the only woman he's seeing?

Do you have Ex's who still call and visit from time to time, but who won't commit to you?

Clear out the Clutter! Make way for the King!

And don't be selfish; if you normally take up both sides of your double bed, start sleeping on one side in preparation for when he shows up (even though he won't be sleeping there for the first three months at least).

If your wardrobe is bursting with clothes, make a space for him to hang his clothes.

Learn how to cook (if you don't know).

Learn about the benefits of aromatherapy oils and massage.

Start a Self-development program.

These are just some of the things you can do to prepare yourself.

Where Can You Meet a 'Good Black Man'?

♥ Black film/cinema clubs

♥ Cultural events

♥ Poetry events

♥ Book Clubs

♥ Meetup Events

♥ Weddings

♥ Funerals

♥ Christenings

♥ Church

♥ Discussion Forums

♥ Book Signing Events*

Ladies, there's no point in moaning and complaining that you can't find a man if all you do is go to work and come home again. You've got to put yourself 'out there' and get to places where you're likely to meet one! Note how I did NOT mention nightclubs. So if all you do is go to work, come home, and go to nightclubs at the weekend, there lies your problem. If you're looking for your soul mate, you have to get out to the places where you're likely to meet him. In 2010 I organised two events: *'What Black Men Want'*, and *'What Black Women Need'*, where the men had the opportunity to tell the women what they wanted in a relationship, and visa versa. Both events were packed. I used the information I received from the two events and fed them into my Self-help novel; when I did the Book Launch for *'Single, Spiritual…AND Sexual!'* on 2nd December 2012, an equal balance of men and women attended. I guess the men knew there were going to be Single, Spiritual…AND Sexual women there, and wanted to meet them! I think book-signing events are a good way to meet like-minded people, and I'm committed to using any ones I organise to give us the opportunity to *talk to each other, meet and mingle, dance and get to know each other*, so they will also double up as a networking events!

Be Open!

Now, when he shows up he may or may not look like what you imagined. For example, he may not have a job, but he may have a brilliant idea for a business, or he may be earning less than you, but he may be a good cook. Or he may not look exactly like how you were visualising. Be open!

"Treat each man as special. Imagine buying a jacket you really like from a second hand shop; you just love it. Buying a used car it will seem normal to ask for the history, unlike the jacket you'll create your own history. Therefore with the man you choose, you care about him, protect him, gradually love grows and a new HISTORY is born" ~ **Clarence Davies** aka **Freestyle**

The last brother I 'dated' (I say it in inverted commas because we hardly went on dates as he wasn't working) loved going to the park and feeding the ducks and squirrels. I love the park too, so it was nice to meet someone who shared my love for nature. Even though he couldn't afford to take me out as much as he might have liked to, he enjoyed cooking for me. Now I'm not going to lie, cooking and cleaning is not one of my favourite things to do. I find it quite boring and laborious – and after you've done it, it's all got to be done again! At least when I write or paint it's there forever...so one day I went to an African market and picked up this lovely kente cloth apron. When I next visited him I gave it to him. He put it on and went straight into the kitchen and made me a meal. Now that's what I'm talking about! I can already hear the brothers saying I'm 'de-masculating' them, but in my experience, men who can cook generally do it better than me, and I personally am *not* going to fight them for that role. If he cooks, I'll wash up (even though I don't particularly like that role either). I might as well let y'all know now; when it comes to domestics, I am not 'The One', especially when I'm in Creative Mode – don't even ask me to do menial tasks like cooking and cleaning. My sons used to call me lazy because I would make them do the shopping and most of the housework. They would see me relaxed on the sofa a lot. They didn't realise that in order for me to access my 'higher mind', I have to be in a state of total relaxation.

Learn each other's strengths and weaknesses, and work with them.

Be Prepared to Invest in Him

A MAN
WITH DREAMS
NEEDS
A WOMAN
WITH VISION.
Her perspective, faith, and support will change his reality. If she doesn't challenge you, then she's no good for you. Men who want to stay ordinary will tell you not to have expectations of them. Men who want to be great will expect you to push them, pray with them and invest in them.

When I say 'invest' in him, I mean your time AND money (if need be). Our brothers need help, even the ones who are working.

In order to heal our relationships we have to do it *together*. You must look for the *potential* in him. As Muhammad Ali put it *'A man without vision has no wings'* If he has vision and ambition, work with him and help him realize his goals.

'Wings of an Eagle' by Cezanne

'The System' has done its best to try to 'clip the wings' of our Black men, but *we* can help put them back together again. If you know the ancient Egyptian story of Ausar and Auset, it was *her* job to find the scattered pieces of her murdered husband and 'resurrect' him. The only part she couldn't find was his penis (the word 'erection' is derived from the word 'resurrection'), yet she was still able to impregnate herself. This is symbolic. Help your man to fly if you can; help put him back together again. He has a hard enough time *outside* of the home; make your home a safe haven for him to *want* to come home to.

Advice from the Brothers

I asked a number of Black Men: What advice can you give to our sisters who are seeking to meet and marry a good Black Man (or get their man to commit)

This is some of their advice:

"To look no further than the values they would raise their own sons to have, their fathers to have shown, and their brothers to have given. If they demand that in the men they wish to be in their lives, their work is almost done" ~ **Jide Oriogun** aka **Knee Deep**

"All Black men are good. All of them. Every single one. Just as there are different grades of steel for different industrial and commercial functions, there are different grades of physical strength, intellect and intelligence for different life challenges, so it depends upon what you want to produce; you would not use cutlery grade steel for skyscrapers (and aeroplanes require a different alloy altogether!)

If you want to produce children, any man who has looked after his physical and emotional health will suffice. If you want to live comfortably in the Western world, a man with intelligence/ability to earn £60,000 pa – with or without you – is requisite. If you want to build a nation, and heal a community, cultural awareness and spiritual connections are important so just as you blend carbon, iron, and time to make steel, you can actively blend these qualities in ALL the men you meet, and then this circle of men will, in my experience, attract through the individual partner or partners you want/need to learn what it is you need to learn. A good Black man is a means to wealth, not riches itself (by wealth I simply mean the number of phone calls required to realise your dream(s) and by riches, I mean material, manifest goods that liberate or enable).

We know that many of our Black women in diaspora have partnered or have been partnering with low grade men to produce high grade children; this is not impossible, but unnecessarily difficult in any case, there is little sense in berating the Black man for being at the grade he is at; as with the steel, the correct additives must be added at the correct time to get the strength/consistency, flexibility required".

~ **Vidal Montgomery**, Professional Double Bass player (photo also contributed by Vidal*)*

What Advice Can I Give To Our Sisters Who Are Seeking To Meet And Marry A Good Black Man? By Kwame McPherson

"As I write I question how one can define who is a 'Good Black Man'?

Is there a differentiation between what is good versus what is bad? And what is that definition? What does he look like? Or is it that Brothers themselves are on a journey of seeking their own truth and as such, enter relationships whether sexual or emotional where the Sister herself is also finding out who she is?

I have always wondered about the term, 'a good Black Man', its perception and the perspective.

Is it that Black Men who know themselves, are responsible, considerate, committed, strong, compassion, honest, hardworking and so on are deemed 'A Good Black Man'? Or is it that there are so few of us Black Men who depict all of who a Black Man should be? Even then, what does that look like?

I must say I found it challenging to formulate advice for Sisters on what counts as a Good Black Man, much less on how to seek and marry one. Every woman will have her own measuring stick on what that looks like. Plus with everybody carrying with them their own stuff, focusing on Brothers is a tad unfair. Sisters need to look at themselves too.

There is no prescriptive formula that will enable Sisters to meet and marry a Brother. Einstein once defined madness as: 'If you keep doing the same thing over and over and expect a different result.' With that said what have Sisters changed to make things happen for them?

So I have tried to list (not exhaustive) what I think a Sister must be and know when seeking a Brother:

* Come from a position of self worth and self love – when you value yourself, someone will value you.

* Do be grounded – that is know who you are, where you're going and what your principles and ethos are. Respect yourself. If you decide to give up the coochie, make sure it's from a position of choice and everybody is clear about what it is and not what you think it is!

* Do be patient – let him wait. If you're worth his salt, he will wait as long as he can to be with you. If he's only after one thing, he'll eventually show his hand and may move on. But remember, 'patient man ride donkey' or a man will find you to be a conquest and will wait you out. You have been warned.

* Focus on you, your dreams and goals – don't worry about tomorrow, it will take care of itself.

* There must be compatibility and this is goes beyond the physical. Chemistry is also important since this will help going through the rough times. It doesn't make sense being with someone for the sake of it.

* Don't be in a hurry to find love – that's when the mistakes occur, since everything that comes your way will look like the 'one', only for you to be disappointed. Take your time. Find YOU first. Then he'll find you!

* Don't believe that you're too old to find love or 'the one' – like above; every person is on their own journey. When you are ready within yourself, you'll find the one – as a matter of fact, he'll find you.

* Don't be distorted by lyrics, sweet talk, and materialism or be driven by societal definitions of who a Black Man should be – this is a misconception. Not all Brothers are tall, dark and handsome, like a Denzel or Idris; nor do they own a yacht or drive a Bentley car like a Foxx.

* Don't think you'll find a 'good Black man' in a nightclub – if that's your interest fine but be warned many Brothers go to nightclubs to have fun, not to find a wife (not saying that doesn't happen, question is, will it happen to you?).

* Don't give up the coochie (unless you feel you want or need to) too quickly – if he's worth his weight in wanting to be with you, he'll wait. If not, he'll eat and run (pardon the pun!). Sometimes resulting in an unwanted expectation in the sound of little feet!

* Don't build a relationship based on lust – it will never last (though there maybe the odd exception to this rule).

* Do go to places where you are intellectually challenged – such as the theatre, museum, art galleries, libraries, meetup events; guarantee that you will find someone who stimulates the cerebral. If that is not your thing, no problem, just be aware of where you go and who you're attracting. That will be a big indicator.

* And finally, just be true to yourself. A lifelong marriage and the ring will all come when and if it comes." ~ **Kwame M.A. McPherson** © Oct 2013 (Authorprenuer/Poet/Writer)

"What advice can I give to women seeking to meet and marry their soul mate?
Meeting such a person is never easy and should be expected to

take a little time but I'd say; sign up to a good dating website (not free) as one way to screen as many guys as possible and to assess how they present themselves. Also, talk to men that do everyday jobs but that seem to have that little extra about themselves. Allow friends to introduce you to someone that they think you might like and vice versa. Clubs... Not really best places as a bit hit and miss (especially for girls trying to find guys).

Church... Maybe.

Once found or screening... Keep it real! Do as you feel and don't moderate too much! By that I mean don't <u>not</u> do something because you think it too soon or set things to occur only when you dictate. Sex is best gotten out the way early (only if you feel that chemistry exists strongly between you) because the longer it is left, the more pressure, tension, expectation it builds. Sometimes that can be good but other times it can also be very bad and majorly anti-climatic which you don't want (or him for that matter). I say, if it's clear that's all a guy wants from you is sex then give him nothing! But if you happen to be speaking to a man who is sharing the clear plans that he has for himself and through talking you both see where you could both feature as a complement to each other then you decide if anything should happen before time.... Finding someone that wants to be a complement to your life is hard...

And equally someone who knows themselves and who is always prepared to engage in direct, honest communication (even in the face of a disagreement)... Is tough.

And not to mention... To find that same someone that ignites and stirs you passionately just at the mere thought of them (and you and all you might do).... Who is committed to evolving, growing and maturing through each and every experience is challenging.... But anyway.... (note: some of my soulmate criteria)...

Let's presume you have found such a person.

"How can you best prepare yourself to be ready to receive your soul mate?

Know yourself as completely as possible. Work to positively address any negative traits within your character. Be clear about what type of contribution you want your man to make in your life and then encourage him to do so. Be loving, be selfless (to a point), be respectful (at all times regardless of circumstance). Keep an open mind and always strive to be the best version of yourself you can be firstly for you...then your man.

Getting that ring on your finger is just the beginning... That's when the journey actually begins.....
Wishing each of you love & happiness along your quest" ~ **Byron**, married father of two

"Get to know him before you let your emotions take over and you decide to sleep with him. Make sure the brother either has ambition or is in something already. And make sure there's some kind of venture (business or otherwise) that you can both work on as a couple to maintain the bond." ~ **Minty**, Nubia House Radio

"Learn who men are, and the way we are in this society, and give them space to be men in the way they want to be. The traditional male role has been chipped away at. It needs to be re-inforced. On the flip side, women have to know themselves and what they're looking for. Look at the wider implications of Black men in the UK and the challenges we face, e.g. Black men are not respected compared to other men, by the way they are portrayed in the media. Black men are not allowed to exert their warrior spirit. If that is not understood, it can seep into the relationship. When coming into relationships, scale down your list of aspirations. Whatever you're looking for in a man, you must reflect those qualities yourself". ~ **James**

"Women are more drawn to cultural things than men, so they need to know what kind of man they are looking for. At the same time, men need to understand that women are our mothers (from an ancestral point of view) when dealing with women, we need to remember that they could be our mother, sister or daughter, so we have to look after and respect them. This is a word to the females as well, that they need to know that nobody comes unto the planet unless through them. This is part of Yoruba culture. It's the mother that nurtures the child, the first teacher is always the

mother. If you can't love your mother, you can't love anybody else. Within Yoruba culture women learn how to look after children, cooking, giving advice, patience, unconditional love, growing up in preparation to becoming a partner. We have to stop trying to copy European culture. Move away from Eurocentric feminism and embrace our own culture. Women should not chase men. The women should show signals to the man that she is interested and let the man do the chasing". ~ **Kolade**, Teacher: Learn Yoruba in London

"Coming from an Afrikan perspective, the advice I would give to the empresses of today is to first; understand the concept of marriage and look at it beyond a ceremony of being in church, wearing a long white wedding dress and signing 'SO-CALLED' legal documents. Marriage is, and should be a spiritual bond between the 2 sexes. As an Afrikan man I think that a spiritual bond between someone you wish to share the rest of your life with is more important and meaningful than trying to follow the Western society tradition. We don't need to be living in a Walt Disney fairy tale, which causes confusion living in an illusion.

It doesn't mean by doing it that way that your man will stick by you or not cheat. The misconception a lot of women who were either born or live in the UK feel that if a man is not marrying them in the stereotypical Western way then he is known as someone who isn't serious. A man can already take that time to invest into you and create that spiritual connection from just being the father of your child, cooking you food, paying the bills, taking you out or whatever he can contribute by making you feel like the empress you should be. Even by having a child for you and raising the child with you is a form of marriage. Who says you need the slave masters paper to prove that you're married? I'm not trying to say "don't celebrate it as a special day", but be more open minded and create the celebration as your own tradition and not by the laws of the European" ~ ***Suraj**, Seeds of Elevation

"Don't chase the ring, chase the relationship. What does the ring mean? Where did the ring concept come from? Do you want the MARRIAGE or the PERSON? Some women only want

80

marriage because they want to fit into what their mother, grandmother, society tells them to do. Is that person really compatible for you? There's an African saying; 'A bird and a fish can fall in love but they can never build a house together'. When you chase the ring so bad you lose out on the fundamental issues"
~ **Matsinhe**, The Mella Center

"Don't love from outside in, that is LUST so love from inside out that is LOVE, a relationship is like a good dish, (it takes) many ingredients; patience, trust, faith, loyalty, understanding and lots of Love, and before you accept the smallest handcuff in the world (the ring) know it's the right person for the right reason at the right time, then together you can shine, by the Divine, what you have become no longer mine, what's yours is hers, and what's hers is hers, it means if she says no, she can claim rape, once charges pressed prisons sentence you can't escape. Happy relationships"
~ **Jaiyeola Bagbansoro**

"Two words...PAY ATTENTION" ~ **Tony**, married father of four

(I asked "To what?")

"If we have to spell it out, there lies the problem. Women in relationships don't need to be told while single women are always left with questions"

(I've been told!)

"For women looking to marry a good Black Man, my advice is don't 'settle', know what you want in/from that man and stick to your requirements. Accept nothing less. Make a list write down those requirements, be realistic be patient. He will come. Brothers should do the same. Unfortunately we're ruled by emotions and the physical. Once these are put aside and focus is put on what we really want in a spouse, a happy life and fulfilling relationship will be found" ~ **Brian Quavar**, photographer

"The often repeated 'happily ever after' fairy tale ending which presents marriage as the perfect conclusion of any

relationship can be a huge turn off. I like to believe that marriage is like adding permanence to something that is already good and not creating a new relationship of which we have yet to taste. Now of course not every person shares my view, the idea of starting life as a married couple is attractive to many. But I believe that can place a burden of expectation so high that it is only a matter of time before problems occurs. I'm a romantic, as such I wanted to marry a woman I love, am passionate about but equally important, that I had compatibility with and I knew her commitment to both me and our children were proven. Too many of us see marriage as means to prevent loneliness or infidelity. I believe that's a recipe for disaster as both these things can happen inside and outside of wedlock. Some immature men will seek women that desire marriage as a means to prove and maintain an unhealthy dependency - the adoring, submissive trophy wife that satisfies the male ego. These men ultimately want to marry someone like their mother who can treat them like a baby for the rest of their days. Likewise I don't want to become any woman's father figure or absent babyfather.

But just as I am a spiritual being demanding certain chemistry, I am also a physical being requiring a woman who treats me like a man, and a political being desiring a woman who values herself with a level of cultural consciousness. Someone who makes me feel at home when we're together just chillin', the feminine Oshun to my masculine Ogun. If we are constantly arguing, I am not going to want to spend the rest of my life in conflict. If simply looking at you, even when asleep makes me smile, I'm going to want to take hold of you and grow old with you. Hence my advice to those wanting to know what makes a man like me place a ring on a woman's finger and say 'I do' – it's knowing that her confidence in us mean she wants to get married but doesn't feel we need to just to keep us together. For me that willing inter-dependency is like a drug of the highest spiritual potency."
~ **Toyin Agbetu**, Ligali

"*What kind of relationship does he have with his parents?*"
~ **Garry Grant**, entrepreneur

"When looking for a husband you must look into his background; if he grew up seeing his parents in a happy marriage it would determine his own views on marriage" ~ **Bunmi**

"Observe how they treat their mother, sister and siblings. Be friends for the first 6 months. When he's talking to you is he looking at your eyes or your breasts?" ~ **Rudolph Mendoza,** sculptor (In other words, if a man cannot be seen to be loving and respectful to his own mother, what makes you think he's going to treat *you* any better?)

"Hi Cezanne, thank you for contacting me. To be honest I'm not sure if I am the right person to ask as I am STILL trying to find a nice woman myself.
But as you have asked I will do my best: Perhaps spend some more time around men and get to understand how we think. Not to say we do not have feelings, but men tend to look at things logically and go by how they THINK. Generally speaking we are not as emotional as women (I know I am generalising here). When communicating with a man it is better to be more LITERAL and DIRECT in what you are trying to get across (that doesn't mean be rude and that applies to both genders). If I ask you what is wrong and you say "nothing" I am hearing the literal word "nothing", so I will think nothing is wrong, even though that may not be what you mean. Two last points, if you want to know a good man, look at the way how he treats his mother. Also if we are stressed, we NEED silence. When we are ready we will come and talk to you."
~ **Dennis Brown**, Amelu Arts

"Love can change colours so learn to love in the day or night"
~ **Edward Ofosu**, Artist

In other words, it won't always be bright and colourful, you're going to have those grey days. When you're going through the rough times, take off the rose-coloured glasses and deal with the reality of the situation.

In **Year Seven** of *'Single, Spiritual...AND Sexual!'* I was given a beautiful analogy to share about relationships:

'Relationships have their seasons; just as there is Summer, Autumn, Winter and Spring, relationships also go through their seasons – it can't always be Summer. There are also the cold winter months when it seems as if everything has died, but in Spring everything starts to blossom, and before you know it, it's Summer again! The problem is, most people give up during their 'winter period', thinking the relationship has died...'

So then I asked: "What would make YOU want to put a ring on a woman's finger?"

"What would make me put a ring on a woman's finger starts with LOVE. We would have to get along really well. It would need to be a relationship that works in terms of compatability and good communication. We should be able to compromise when it is required as each other's differences on life and for us both to be free to be individuals as well as soul mates. I think that feeling of putting a ring on her finger means I'm at home with this lady. She makes me feel whole and complete. She gives me a great feeling of joy that I don't want to let go of and can't get enough of. Such feelings of happiness, Love, joy, freedom, fulfilment all those beautiful feelings and oneness.. She's a person who's a friend and lover... All these beautiful feelings have developed through months and time spent together have now led us both and me to the point where I now feel to get down on one knee and ask for hand in marriage and get the ring on her finger" ~ **Carl Foster**, Author of Selfmade

"This is very poignant as I recently committed, but now have reservations...but what made me commit was honesty, support, and interest in/respect for my children. Most of all the man will only commit if he feels the commitment will inspire and help him grow. Obviously she must also be a good woman" ~ **Trevor**

"What made me decide to put a ring on my wife's finger was that she understood me, I thought we could work together, and there was compatibility. She took the time to learn who I was.

84

And of course, I loved her" ~ **James**, aka Buzzing Bee, SLR Radio

"Simply put, being or feeling in love and being ready to make a commitment. How does a woman know when a man is ready to make such a commitment? By simply asking him! Age can and does play a part in that readiness however since (as in my case) when I was in my early 20's I definitely was not ready but 10 years later I was.
What made me put a ring on my wife's finger? I felt ready to make that commitment, I felt I had found someone I could grow with and who was committed to evolving. And I was ready to put in the work needed to give my marriage every chance for success" ~ **Byron**, married father of two

"What would make me put a ring on the finger, is an empress who is loyal and sees potential in me and doesn't disconnect after the first hurdle. Someone who is into the same things as me or at least has an interest. A woman who is supportive and doesn't just think about herself. Someone who is driven towards success. A beautiful empress who knows about her history and knows how to express her feelings. Someone who is understanding and knows how to conduct herself in the general public, a woman who can be a good mother to my children and is family orientated. Last, but not least. A sister who is connected with her roots is very important to me and is my potential queen to be" ~ **Suraj**, Seeds of Elevation

Do You Have a Plan?

'Know Your Plan' by Nigel Beckles

'Do you want to be in a committed relationship or to be married? Have you got a plan to make this happen? Many women make the big mistake of not saying upfront what they expect from a relationship and find themselves resenting their partner because he won't make a firm commitment after months or even years!

Your plan should be **SMART**:

Specific – Do you want a committed relationship or do you want to be married?

Measurable – How long will you date before expecting a commitment?

Achievable – Are your expectations reasonable and achievable?

Realistic – Are your timescales realistic?

Timely – Is your goal timely (you are not expecting a man to propose within 2 months!)

Every relationship is different but generally after 2/3 months of dating (dating defined as getting to know a man without sexual relations) you should both know whether you want to pursue an exclusive, committed relationship or not. If marriage is a woman's goal this should be discussed at the beginning. Many women make the mistake of assuming a wedding will happen eventually. Generally, after year one and no longer than 18 months of a relationship wedding plans should be discussed providing there are not any major issues. Research indicates if after three years of being in a relationship and marriage has not taken place it is unlikely to ever happen'.

© **Nigel Beckles**, extract from his book '*How to Avoid Making The BIG Relationships Mistakes!*' due for publication early 2014

"Have we gone backwards?

Women, you can't give a man the following options:
a) sex without commitment.
b) continued sex without commitment and a child is born.
After he exercises the options YOU gave him, you offer an ultimatum "Marry me or else". I mean really. NOW you want to be someone's wife, NOW you want discipline, now you want commitment AFTER all that required all the above has already taken place. This is what we should say in the FIRST place if that is our true desire. It's like giving a child dessert first, then complaining at the fact that he won't eat his vegetables! BACKWARDS!" ~ **Ms K. Armstrong** (posted on FB)

Alex Burnett, who has been with his wife for 30 years (married for 27) gave this advice:

"Make it clear to him from day one what you want from the relationship. If it's marriage, children and to own your own home let him know. This could be very off-putting for some men but at least you will know whether or not he was serious about you. (This is not to say that you would like all of the above today). Some men because they've been hurt in the past may be reluctant to tie the knot and by you showing your intentions may put his mind at ease"

It's not often that we talk about how the breakup of a relationship affects the man. But sometimes men are 'dumped' just when they were beginning to or had already fallen deeply in love with the woman. Have you ever dumped a man just in case he ends it with you first, just to protect your own feelings? I know I have. But it's time to grow up, and be clear right from the beginning of the relationship about what you want so that you *both* know where you stand.

That leaves me pondering; if a man and a woman are *both* going into a relationship with feelings of inadequacy, Self Love issues, jealous and possessive tendencies, they are already starting off on the wrong foot.

Each person should come into the relationship as a whole person. When two whole people who know themselves, know what they want out of life, and are clear about the type of person they want to join themselves to *meet*, the relationship stands a much better chance of being successful.

DIY Arranged Marriage

Back in the day, before the enslavement and Colonialism of Africans by Westerners, our *parents* would have been involved in our courting. The father would 'interview' the young man to see if he was going to be good husband material for his daughter before dating could even commence.

Both parents played an active role in making sure their daughter was treated right during the courtship. And after 6 months if no proposal had been offered, they would want to know *why*.

Some people think that love has to be there right from the beginning – love at first sight. However in ancient times before a man and woman were declared fit for marriage many things were taken into consideration, e.g. their family histories, astrological and numerological dates etc. They did not marry because they were 'in love', they married because they were well suited to each other. Love grew later. In the Asian culture this is still practiced today (I wonder where they learnt that from?)

Nowadays, it's hit and miss. You start a relationship and it appears that you both have lots in common. You jump into bed with him because you think he's 'The One'. Three months later the cracks begin to show. You begin arguing. You suddenly realise that you didn't have as much in common as what you first thought. 6 months later the relationship either comes to an end, or you stay in it rather than being alone, even though you're unfulfilled.

These days people aren't taking the time to really get to know each other properly before committing their bodies; they are literally 'sleeping with a stranger'. As a result of writing my Self-help novel *'Single, Spiritual...AND Sexual!'* I would now find it very difficult to just jump into bed with any man. Or maybe I've just wised up. Age is a wonderful thing. I don't know why people are so 'anti-ageing'. With age comes experience, and with experience, wisdom.

So since there's no-one there to arrange your marriage for you, you're going to Do It Yourself. Yes, a **DIY Arranged Marriage!** From now on, any man who wants to date me has to read this book first. Make life easier for your Self and do the same thing, that way you'll both be on the same page right from the beginning. If he's serious about you, he'll go along with it. If not, let him be.

What Does a 'DIY Arranged Marriage' Consist Of?

It starts with the **6 Month Test**, which is broken down into two stages: the **First Three Months**, and the **Last Three Months**.

During the first three months of dating, your job is to find out as much about your potential husband as possible. Avoid getting 'emotionally involved' at this stage; you're just taking time to get to know each other.

You should be having NO SEX for *at least* the first three months of your relationship. The idea is to build intimacy, and get to know each other properly before committing your body. If you've only just met, it's best to wait the whole 6 months before having sex.

Even after 3 months you're still getting to know each other, you're still in the 'honeymoon period' of your relationship, where everything looks rosy and the sun shines out of the other person's backside. You're still getting butterflies every time you hear his voice, you smile every time you think about him or get a text from him etc. BUT….you are still getting to know him. He's still wearing the mask in most cases. And so are you. The real test comes AFTER the 6 months, or ultimately when you start *living together*. So don't rush into jumping into bed with him, take the necessary time to get to know him properly first. Sex can wait. In fact, the longer you make him wait, the better. I know this is difficult when the attraction is strong, so what do you do to avoid making that mistake?

Avoid Spending Time Alone Together in the First 3 Months

That's right, go out instead!

Go to the park, go out for a meal or a drink, go shopping together, go sightseeing together, go on a train ride out of town (or by car – but keep your hand off his gear stick!), go to the cinema or theatre etc.

If you get past the first hurdle, move on to the second stage: In the last 3 months you can begin getting intimate, meet friends and family, sleep over at each other's places and hopefully, you'll both be ready for a more longer term commitment – marriage.

(N.B. when I say 'marriage', I'm not just talking about the 'White Wedding'. You must both establish what marriage means to you.

For me, marriage is nothing to do with a white dress, signing a 'contract', or the honeymoon; it's a marriage of our *minds*).

As part of your personal evolution, this is something that you're going to teach to your *children* so that the next generation don't make the same mistakes we've made. What we're aiming to do is **break the psychological programming handed down to us through our DNA by the slave master**.

Your 6 Month Test might look something like this:

First 3 Months	Month 1	Month 2	Month 3
	Meet face to face/Phone Conversations/ First Date/Build Friendship	Find out as much about the person as possible/Talk about everything, including sex!	First Kiss, Meet the Family & Friends/Plan when you will consummate your relationship (have sex) STD Tests
Last 3 Months	**Month 4**	**Month 5**	**Month 6**
	Sleepovers for pillow talk, massage, getting to know each other's bodies	Spend weekends/weeks together to see if you can 'live together'/Plan your moving in together	Consummation of relationship/Some form of commitment in the way of a ring? plans to move in together, or whatever you both agreed upon in the beginning

If he gets past the first 3 months, then you can start introducing him to friends and family.

Now don't get me wrong, you're not looking for a man who shows no interest in you sexually at all, he just has to be able to hold it down (literally!). Brothers who have no Self-control are the ones who will be more likely to cheat on you. If he can't wait

6 months, what's he going to do when you're pregnant with his child, or just had his baby for instance?

So the 6 Month Test is to test his *will-power*. A man with a weak will-power is like a muscle that hasn't been exercised: Flabby and Weak. Do you know any men like that? I do. So what we're looking for is a strong Black brother, or one who's *willing* to develop his will-power.

Now if you're thinking this is all about him, you're wrong. Are YOU a strong Black woman? Now when I say STRONG, I don't mean the "I don't need a man" type. I mean the type of Strong Black Woman who knows what she wants and knows how to get it. Do you know how to get the ring on your finger?

Remember, this book is just a guide, it's not a step-by-step manual; I'm not telling you what to do, I'm just giving you the best chance of getting the ring on your finger. My aim is not to spell everything out to you; you have your own inner guide as well.

So let's assume that you came to one of my Book-Signing Events and you met someone. You already have a head-start, because he will already be on the same page as you; you both have the *intention* of meeting your soul mate and getting *married*.

The first thing you want to establish is that. You're not looking to waste your time dating lots of men who are just in it for fun.

Once you've checked each other out and there's a connection/attraction, spend time in conversation. Initially, this should be face to face, and then over the phone. Spend at least two weeks getting to know each other over the phone before you go on your First Date. Find out as much as possible about each other.

Why over the phone?

You need to give the relationship time to grow into a *friendship* before it turns into a *relationship*. Don't even think of him as a 'potential' at this point. Don't get emotionally involved!

Just use the time to get to know each other. This is only the first rung up the Ladder to Dating Success.

Ladder to Dating Success

Month 6 – Solid Commitment in the way of a Wedding Proposal, or other plans to unite.

Month 5 – Spend Weekends and Weeks Together (take turns with whose place you stay at)

Month 4 – Sleepovers/Get to Know Each Other's Bodies Through Massage

Month 3 – Introduce to Friends & Family/First Kiss/Plan First Night Together

Month 2 – Dig Deeper; find out their history, inc. financial

Month 1 – Get to Know Each Other as Friends/Go on Dates/Dinner/Phone Calls

Things you should be looking for could be:

- ♥ Can he communicate openly with you?

- ♥ Does he keep his phone on silent when he's with you?

- ♥ Is he unavailable at certain times (e.g. evenings/weekends)

- ♥ Is he attentive to you (both indoors and out)

- ♥ Does he have his own interests? (apart from football and going out drinking with his friends)

- ♥ Is he on his own personal development journey?

- ♥ Does he use every opportunity to try and get you into bed?

Find out each other's history (work, family, relationships, children, education, likes/hobbies/interests, future plans, ambitions, dreams etc).

Are there any similarities? For example, he may dream of immigrating to another country; was that part of your plans, and if not, would you be happy to go along with that? Does he have children already? If so, would you be happy to incorporate them into your life together? Do you have similar interests? For example, do you both like reading/shopping/going out/staying in/the theatre/exercising/eating healthily/spiritual matters/cultural events etc.

Once you have established that you have enough in common and want to take it further, plan your First Date. This doesn't have to be anything costly. If the weather's nice, go to the park, or sightseeing, or just find somewhere where you can go for a quiet meal and drink (not yours or his place).

Communication is the Key!

"Get to know each other first. Take time to talk; people are always talking about talking but don't know what it means.
~ **Bunmi**

If he can get through the tough questions and still be eager to pursue a relationship with you, that's a good start. Don't be afraid to ask!

'...Are you my soul mate?
The One with whom I can share a deep, spiritual
connection?
Are you looking for True Love or just a One Night Stand?
Can we talk freely? And will you open up to me completely
Because communication is the key....'

(Extract from **R U 'The One'**? on the Seeds of Love CD)

"Building Functional Adult relationships has to come to the center of focus for our collective culture. Functional Adult relationships require high level communication skills and the ability to engage in complex streams of consciousness like Self-examination, sacrifice, and loyalty. As a group we must begin

to pursue collective goals for our culture and building functional adult relationships as Black men and women must be at the top of our list of goals" ~ **Morpheus Prime** (Google+)

What Should You Talk About?

The **Relationships Advice Hangout Community** on FB said to ask these Questions:

Are you comfortable talking about where our relationship is going?

Are you ready to commit to me?

Are you happy with me?

Why did your last relationship end? How did you cope with it?

What have you learned from your last relationship?

Do you want to marry me someday?

Do you want to change anything in this relationship?

How are we going to handle the finances if we live together?

Have you ever got physically abusive?

Who will we spend holidays with when we are married?

If one of my friends flirted with you, would you tell me?

How far apart in age would you like your children to be?

When do you see yourself having children?

How many children would you like to have someday?

How would you deal with a disagreement with one of my family members or friends?

Are you close to your parents?

Everyone has regrets about their past. Which is the one thing in your past you would like to change?

What according to you is a perfect life, and how you would you try to make it for yourself and me?

Are you a person who keeps enemies, grudges or any negative thoughts about a person?

If I were offered a promotion and had to move away, would you move with me?

This is just a guide, have fun with it! Alter the questions to suit yourself, but make it a point to find out some key things about him/her right from the start (so you don't waste your time).

I remember when 'H' asked me out on our first date back in 2001. When I told him I was going to have a list of questions for him he replied "Yeah, I bet you're going to laminate them as well!" So I did.

Ladies,

When a man speaks of his pending future i.e. marriage & family

And you're nowhere to be found in the vision,

Well, let's just say

"HE'S NOT THAT INTO YOU"

(FB Group: Courtship vs. Dating)

Talk About Everything, including Sex!

Earlier this year I was building up a friendship with 'C'. I'd already known him a few years, but it was only in the last year that he moved into my 'inner circle'. We both have a love for nature so we would meet up and go to the park to feed the ducks and squirrels, if it was hot we would sit on the grass and toast ourselves in the sun, or watch the sun set. We would then go back to his place and watch DVD's together and just enjoy chilling in each other's company.

After some months of this, I began to develop feelings for him so told him (in a text). He sent me one back saying that I could stay over at his place and we could get up early and go to the park to feed the ducks, but that was all he could offer me at that time. Fair enough.

That night we stayed up late watching DVD's and chatting. Actually, now I think about it, 'C' wasn't a brilliant communicator, which I'm guessing maybe the reason why he played one DVD after the other.

But he became a different person in bed. He would talk for England. I think he felt more relaxed there. So it was in bed that I really got to know the real 'C'.

I stayed over at his place on a number of occasions, but we never had sex. During our 'pillow talk' we frolicked and messed about with each other, but we never kissed or 'went all the way' (more about that later). While we were 'getting to know each other' I found out that there were certain things he wouldn't do in bed, calling them 'deviant Western practices'. Now either he's wrong or my spirit guides are wrong, but while doing the research for *'Single, Spiritual…AND Sexual!'* I learnt that those same 'devious Western practices' actually *empower* a man! (And no, I'm not talking about anal sex – that *is* a deviant Western practice!)

I also learnt from our 'pillow talk' that 'C' wanted to start a family. Since I'd already made my contribution to the world's population, this wasn't something I could help him with, and so there really wasn't any point in taking the relationship any further.

Talking about what you would and wouldn't do in bed is important, before you get there!

Dig Deeper

I'm assuming that your First Date went well, and you've established that you want to pursue a relationship. The most important thing is communication. Relationships break down because of lack of it. Both of you should be making an effort to be open and honest with each other.

Is he being open and communicative with you? If he lacks communication skills, create an atmosphere that encourages open communication. Cook him a candle-light dinner. Now if you're going to be inviting him around for dinner in the first three months, make sure that you are both in agreement that he's not going to stay over late; he should be getting ready to leave by 10pm. The longer he stays past this time, the more likely the chance he'll end up staying, and that's a no-no!

Anything that's going to divert your attention away from each other should be banned. Don't allow the t.v. to invade on the time you should be spending engaging in quality time talking to each other. Turn it off! Low music in the background is better, and sets the scene for some good conversation.

"Each time a man looks into your eyes, he is only searching to find himself, for he already knows that he is part of you"

Is he engaging in eye-to-eye contact? If he doesn't allow you to look deep into his eyes (the windows to his soul) he might have something to hide.

Is he serious about you?

Don't ignore any tell-tale signs that may be telling you something's not quite right. When a man is into you, you can tell.

Don't be so desperate to get a ring on your finger that you don't take the time to get to know the brother properly.

Some years ago I learnt from first-hand experience about a whole different group of men:

On the Downlow?

There are men who will have their girlfriend/wife but are secretly having sex with other men. I'm not going to go into too much detail about this, but BE AWARE that there are men who will be looking for a wife and to create a family just so they can have their 'front', when really they're into men.

How can you tell?

Does he have an unhealthy relationship with another man? e.g. his 'friend' is always round his house, or they insist on doing a lot of things together.

They are generally into sports, e.g. football, or maybe into the current hip-hop culture (I'm not saying all Black men into hip-hop sleep with other men!).

Everything is Energy

Another reason for doing the **6 Month Test** is that if either you or him has had sex with someone else recently (within the last 6 months) the 'residue' of the other person will still be lurking. Everything is energy, and spiritually having sex (or making love) transfers your essence unto him, and visa versa. Have you ever felt drained of your energy after making love? Beware the Vampire! Now I know I'm straying from the point I was going to make, but I just wanted to talk a bit about *energy vampires*. Have you ever experienced your energy being drained after making love? In my poem *'Beware the Vampire!'* I'm warning the sisters about these types of men, and what to look out for. I tend to avoid men who display vampire traits these days. How will you recognize one? Listen to the poem! (on my CD *'Rise of the Phoenix'*). So let me get back to the point: When you have sex with someone you're also sharing your energy on a *spiritual* level. When a woman has sex with a man, she's looking for love (no matter how casual she may try to be about it). When a man has sex with a woman in most cases he's not looking past that (unless he's clued up to all this stuff). If you're looking for LOVE, don't use SEX as a tool to get it – it just doesn't work! Don't say you're happy to just be in a sexual relationship with him if you're HOPING it will lead to LOVE and MARRIAGE – it just doesn't work! Now of course there are exceptions to this rule, but I'm speaking generally here.

Don't Be Needy!

Now that you've established a relationship, don't be needy! Remember, you are two individual souls on your own soul journeys who have decided to merge at this point in time. Just because he's *in* your life, don't *make* him your life. You should still be pursuing your own interests and personal development. Don't be calling him every minute to find out what he's doing, where he is, who he's with etc. If he's the faithful type, if he loves you, if he's a man of integrity, you won't have to worry about these things, and if he's not, well, there's nothing you can do about it anyway. So why cause yourself unnecessary stress worrying about what he's up to? Focus on your Self! What are YOU doing? What are YOU being? What are YOU having?

In relationships you should always be looking at what you can GIVE, not receive. If you both approach the relationship from that point of view, you will be serving each other well.

Plan Ahead!

If you want children, say so. If you want to buy a house together, say so. If you want to have that male energy around your house, say so. If you want security, say so. If you want *marriage*, say so.

"A woman's natural instinct is to want to pro-create, be loved and feel secure. A sense of security is very important to a woman. If you ask any woman, they would rather have a man around to do certain things. Marriage is a good foundation: Before entering into marriage you should both AGREE what you want out of it. It's like building a building; you don't draw up plans for your building and then change the plan half way through. There are some things that you can change e.g. colours and cosmetics, but the <u>structure</u> of the building must remain the same if you want it to remain intact" ~ **Bunmi**, married father of two

"With Caucasians there's a science to marriage. It's a **contract**. *They are investing their* **time** *and* **money**. *They make sure they're not <u>wasting</u> their time/money, there's a MUTUAL BENEFIT e.g. pro-creating/a merging of wealth)"* ~ **Michael,** BIS Publications

How many couples have opened up a joint bank account with no idea of their partner's financial history, do you think? How many people have gotten into debt because their partners have maxed out credit cards, overspent on unnecessary items, or already had a bad credit history which the other partner now has to deal with?

As part of your **DIY Arranged Marriage**, you are to find out as much about the other person as possible, including their *financial* history (I'm talking to both women *and* men here).

First Kiss

Kissing allows you to assess each other for compatibility, genetic fitness, and general health.

However, men and women don't necessarily view kissing in the same way.

Research suggests that *women* use kissing as a mate assessment device and as a means of initiating, maintaining, and monitoring the current status of their relationship with a *long-term* partner. In contrast, *men* place less importance on kissing, especially with *short-term* partners, and appear to use kissing to increase the likelihood of having sex. (I could have told you that!).

Research also suggests that men and women who rated themselves as being attractive, or who tended to have more *short-term* relationships and *casual encounters*, also saw kissing as *more important*.

Initial attraction might be to do with the face, body and social cues, but the assessments become more and more intimate as we go deeper into the courtship stages, and this is where *kissing* would come in. While a gentle squeeze on the arm or around the shoulder can let people know that you care about each other, a kiss on the lips – even if it's a quick peck in the supermarket – is an internationally understood sign of intimacy.

When is the Right Time to Kiss?

Women rated kissing as especially important in *long-term* relationships, suggesting it also plays a key role in maintaining attachment between *established couples*.

So, as part of your **DIY Arranged Marriage**, you will **refrain from kissing for the first 3 months.**

I hear you gasp in shock and horror, so let me just remind you why you're doing this:

Ok, when I say no kissing I mean 'exchanging of body fluids', so you can kiss on the cheeks, and even (lightly) on the lips – as long as you keep your tongue in your head.

Because once you start mixing body fluids….

Kissing is another level on the ladder to intimacy. Save it for that special day when you decide to move from being friends, to actually courting.

Remember, you're doing a **DIY Arranged Marriage** – you want to get the ring on your finger don't you? So stick to the Plan.

"What if he turns out to be a lousy kisser after waiting the 3 months?"

Well I think it would be safe to say he's likely to be a lousy lover too. And what? You're blaming *me* because you've just wasted 3 months of your life dating a guy only to find out he can't kiss properly? You should be *thanking* me – at least you haven't ended up sleeping with him!

"Is it possible to have 'fun' without having sex?"

The answer to this question is "Yes!"

I *know* it is. I did it with 'C'. We didn't have sex but we DID have fun!

I slept over at his house on a number of occasions and while we built up a level of intimacy, we never had sex.

I have 'C' to thank for being able to say that I've only had one lover in the last 3 years (which just happened to be that same guy I was messing around with on and off for 11 years). 'C' held it down. Literally.

I was just lucky that 'C' was a Self-disciplined brother who had more will-power than me. When I taunted him about being 'virginal' (he's a Virgo) he took offence and said "I went really deep into my Self to show you respect and that's all you can say?" I might not have appreciated his Self-control in the heat of the moment, but I sure do now. He would have just been another 'ex lover' on the list. We're still friends, we just don't frolic anymore.

There aren't that many men with 'C's will-power, so I wouldn't recommend finding out about your prospect from bed.

'...because I'm fed up of jumping into relationships thinking I've met 'The One',
Only to find out 6 months later that; "Oh no, my time with this brother is done!"
In the beginning we thought we had so much in common,
But it wasn't long before the cracks began to show
And we began to grow apart
And before you know it my heart just isn't in it anymore.
So this time, I'm taking my time
We've got to get to know each other properly
Before getting all 'emotionally involved'
To see if we're really compatible,
whether we'll stand the test of time
That's it, just be friends, have fun together
(And you know it is possible to have 'fun' without having sex)
And if he can't wait 6 months that means he's got no control over his physical body
And if he can't control his body he's not the one for me;
I've collected enough Ex's,
Now I'm looking for the one I can spend the rest of my life with'.

(extract from my poem **"I Need a MAN!"**)

If you are physically attracted to each other in a big way and the chemistry is really strong, you'll both have to have a tremendous amount of will-power. But it *can* be done.

The important thing to remember is that you both have to be in AGREEMENT from the beginning. That way, if one of you gets 'weak', the other will remind you of your agreement.

There's nothing wrong with kissing, touching, getting to know each other's bodies through massage etc. (in the second stage of the 6 Month Test) but NO GOING ALL THE WAY!

Things to Do Instead of Having Sex:

- ♥ Pillow Talk. Take time to really get to know each other's *minds* before committing your *bodies.*

- ♥ Massage each other's bodies (massage doesn't have to lead to sex!)

- ♥ Study a good book together that will strengthen your relationship (like this one!)

Massage is a great way to get to know each other's bodies before going all the way. This should be done in the *final stages* of your 6 Month Test. Remember though, the aim is ONLY to get to know each other's bodies. Sometimes people have sex and they haven't even taken the time to explore their lover's body: find out what they like/don't like. Be clear before you begin that this is NOT to lead to sex. The longer you both wait, the better the sex will be (mind you, it could end up being an anti-climax but I think it's still better to wait). I could tell from the way 'C' frolicked with me that he would be a good lover; he was attentive, he talked a lot in bed, he made me laugh. He massaged me (I did offer to do him as well but he refused, saying "My bed, my rules!"). He was willing to open up to me. It's the job of the *brothers* to help the sisters be strong in those weak moments. *He* should be the one reminding you of the agreement you both have, if he has any respect for you. He should WANT this relationship to work. So if you both want to make a success out of your relationship, it shouldn't be all one-sided.

It's not always about sex, sometimes the best type of intimacy is where you just lay back, laugh together at the stupidest things, hold each other, and enjoy each others company...

Something to Look Forward To

Set a Date for when you will finally 'come together' – this should ideally be at the END of the 6 Month Test. Not only will this strengthen your relationship, but it will build intimacy and anticipation for the Big Day. However, if you feel you are both on the same page about where the relationship is going and you have made a solid commitment to each other (and the chemistry is too strong), after 3 months will suffice – but NOT BEFORE THEN!

(Obviously, if you're religiously inclined you shouldn't be going 'all the way' anyway).

I hear some of you saying "Ooooh, this sounds really hard!" But *do you want to get the ring on your finger or not*?

"If he's serious about you he will wait the 6 months. This has been my rule from when I was single. We (men) *do know our boundaries, but we will break them if allowed"* ~**Bunmi**

After the first 3 months, if you're both still into each other, move on to the next stage.

This is where you get to spend cosy evenings in together; take it in turns to stay over at each other's places, don't let it be all one-sided. If he insists on coming to your place all the time, QUESTION IT! Oh yes, he'll have a good excuse, but if you are unable to observe him in his natural environment, you're missing out on a big chunk of getting to know him. Talking to him over the phone for hours does not suffice.

Once you are sure you want to take the relationship to the next level, plan it carefully. Most couples don't plan their first night together, it just 'happens'. You fall in love, you fall out of love again. You fall in bed, you fall out of bed again. One minute you're 'in love' and the sex is great. Then before you know it, just when you thought everything was going great, he ends it, and you wonder what happened?

Eating Peanuts by Toyin Agbetu

As she looked back into him

she recognized he was

her one,

yes he was beautiful

but it was deeper, more romantic

their unquenchable addiction

had taught her

his sensuous touch,

magnificent physique

could not compare to his incredible mind

that vibe when they spiritually dined
entwined, united as one
almost indistinguishable as two
For she admired his soul,
The way he arrogantly always knows her
Inside and out,
Upside and down,
Feeding her,
Loving her
And yet she pondered
Why after three years
Six months
Fourteen days
And nine hours
Why they no longer woke
Nor spoke
Together
Forever
Questioning the cost of their perfection
As he left her for the way she
Noisily
Ate peanuts?

Let Him Be The Man In The Relationship!

If you happen to be earning more than him, it doesn't mean you should try to wear the trousers as well, ALLOW HIM TO BE THE MAN!

Ways you can allow him to be the man:

♥ Don't talk down to him; allow him to feel in control even if you both know he's not

♥ Allow him to fix things around the house even if you can do it yourself

♥ Let him drive your car when you're going out together – if he has a license (put him on your insurance first!)

Two People Both Can't Be Behind The Same Wheel. Each Has A Role To Play In The Relationship. Play Your Role.
www.YouBetterPreach.com

"A lot of feminists are doing things as if to say they are empowering women, but all they're doing is copying what men do; they're playing football, they're boxing, they're doing karate etc. This does not empower women, its turning women further away from their femininity. There are a lot of women that are strangling the female in themselves, locking it up in a room, and they're just being this tough, tough....they LOOK like a woman but they're not FEELING like a woman and not OPERATING like a woman when it comes to interacting with the male energy. And they're encouraging our men to be boys. They're being effeminated, demasculated. And if a man is operating in his masculine energy, you are told to be afraid of it, rather than embrace it. So when you're afraid of something you want to attack it, or defend yourself against it. Then you distort what you think it is. So you're not interacting with the male energy because now it is not being respected. So now it's "He's being aggressive", "He wants to control me"…hang on a second, so if he's being direct because he has his role; he's a penetrative consciousness, women are receptive. We have to understand our bodies; men are positive down below, women are negative. Men are negative in their heart, women are positive. So when we have a proper plug-in (+–, male/female) you get current running through. You get the operation of the whole thing working harmoniously" ~ **Siayoum Atum Ab Ankh Rhem**

"Unity is strength, division is weakness."
~ Swahili Proverb

Don't Blame/Criticize

I know this is a hard one (because we women like to get things off our chest) but don't be talking bad about your man to your girlfriends/family. Work it out together. Only speak words of praise about your man! Thoughts and words are energy. Even when you're going through a rough patch, send out positive thoughts of love to your partner. I do this with my sons and it works. Don't think bad thoughts about your partner, and certainly don't speak evil of them. How do you expect to heal your relationship if you're harming it with negative thoughts and words?

"You can never heal relationships by talking and thinking about how awful it is. The only way you can heal your relationships is by turning your thoughts AWAY from the problems and start creating new thoughts that will produce a solution."

~ Wilfred 'Rawventure' Campbell

108

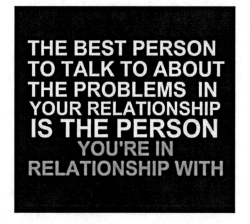

THE BEST PERSON
TO TALK TO ABOUT
THE PROBLEMS IN
YOUR RELATIONSHIP
IS THE PERSON
YOU'RE IN
RELATIONSHIP WITH

Stop Dissing the Brothers!

By 'dissing' I mean dis-respecting (just in case you didn't know).

♥ Don't talk down to him

♥ Don't talk bad about him to your girlfriends/sisters/family/etc.

♥ Praise him when he does something you like

"Encouragement is high on my list. Don't try to assassinate his character" ~ **Wadada** (saxophonist)

Sex is Not to Be Used as a Weapon of Control

"If I'm angry with you today I love you tomorrow. If I hate you today I love you tomorrow, that's what love is. Then you end up using sex to bridge the gap by "Let's fuck and make up" (pardon the pun). When you're having sex without heart-felt love you're contaminating each other. It becomes ego control, when sex is meant to EMPOWER each other. It's about how much you can receive/give FREELY, not "I'll take more but I'm not giving" or "I'll give but I can't receive". Sex shows you where your ego is being the barrier between your free unlimited capacity you have

to give and receive love. So when you come towards sex with a heartful LOVING approach you're actually nurturing and nourishing each other. But when sex is used for manipulation and control, one loses and one gains. So when we talk about the Feminine Energy it's a big, powerful thing we're talking about here. We're not just talking about "You've got breasts, you have a womb, you've got curves, you're a woman". No, that's feminine. That's why people seek to come together, to belong, to feel loved, but in the original impulses of creation, male and female that were in an embrace before the explosion, the Big Bang that separated individually these aspects that came into individualised form. We are individualised consciousness beings coming from the Universal equilibrium that exploded, and so you get this Bang! It's all sexual; if you take your finger and get a seed and plant it in the soil, you finger has to penetrate the soil to plant the seed into it. That's a sexual act" ~ **Siayoum Atum Ab Ankh Rhem**

I asked Siayoum: **"What advice can you give to women to help them balance their feminine energy and bring it into balance with the masculine, in terms of a relationship?"**

*"Firstly, women need to get into a relationship with her Self. How she gets in touch with that feminine aspect of herself it to BE CREATIVE; dance, sing, cook, bake, plant things, nurture them, music, laugh. Stop doing all the logical stuff that men are doing. For a woman to be healthy she needs to know that her strongest polarity is the Feminine, which is creative. The Masculine is also creative but in a different way. They are both creative energies; you have **thought** (male) which is the **image**, and you have **feeling** (female) which is the **water**. Water (woman) receives the impressions; water is impressionable. When the image is impressed upon the feelings, the feelings give form to the thought".*

This reminds me of something: while I was writing my Self-help novel **'Single, Spiritual…AND Sexual!'** in 2011, I woke up in the middle of the night and wrote the scene where the couple performed their first Sex Ritual; the *man* was the one doing the visualisation; he shared his vision with her, then she built up a clear image in *her* mind, and the 'gateway' (which is **in her**)

110

opened, to allow him to '**man**ifest' his desires. A womban's *womb* is able to bring things from the non-physical realm into this physical world, just like babies which are *souls* coming from the spirit realm into this physical world *through her.*

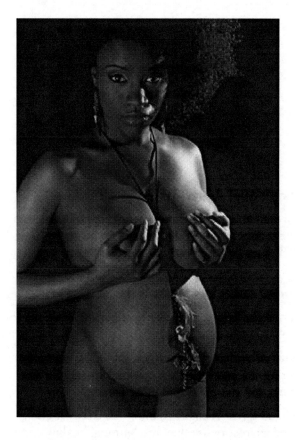

Even as I'm writing *this* book I'm beginning to see an even deeper mystery emerging:

"The word ritual, comes from ritu, meaning "the blood-red",
and the word secret, comes from secretion which implies the
female biological cycle. Moreover, the Egyptian word for
woman was mesta, from which we derive Mystery".
~ Eye 'm King

The Black Man and Womban have the ability to pro-create and bring *anything* from the non-physical realm into this physical world when they come together in a high state of consciousness and perform a Sex Ritual.

Lessons on Sex

Thoughts are energy

Words are energy

Sex is energy

Everything is energy!

SEX, the Spiritual Aspect (taken from Facebook)

When a man enters your womb, what type of energy and consciousness does he have? Is he bitter, is he happy, does he love himself, does he love you? Is he a positive or negative thinker?

When a woman makes love to you is she blessing or cursing you?

Is she bitter, is she happy, does she love herself, does she love you?

Sex is a ritual of exchanging energies, thoughts, emotions and spirits. During sex you become a spiritual sponge for the consciousness and energy of that other person.

Each pump and thrust is an affirmation. Are they draining your life force and energy, or are they re-charging, healing and re-fuelling your spirit?

Be Mindful of the True Power of Sex!

~ Author Unknown

"To understand the masculine and feminine energy, we have to go into **sexual energy**. I find that Black people in general will have a lot of children but don't want to talk about sex. In the back of our minds, we still think it's something dirty, something you mustn't talk about. When you think like that, you don't realise that 80% of people's complexities and psychological issues are to do with suppressed sexuality, and not rightly identifying with your sexual energy, because you're always relating to it like "sex is dirty". Sex is Divine! That's why everybody always says "Oh god, oh god, oh god!" What's God got to do with it when you told me it's a sin? Or "Oh Jesus, Oh God, Oh Jesus!" You know when you're having sex it's sweet, so how can God come into this when you don't even want to admit to anybody that you're having sex or talk about it? You go to church and it's like everybody just came out of an Easter-egg wrapper. Everybody knows you have to have sex to be born, so why are we not looking to understand our approach to our own sexuality, which is our SEXUAL ENERGY,

which is our LIFE FORCE, which is our CREATIVE POWER.
So if you're not embracing and relating to your sexuality and
sexual energy in yourself correctly, how can you even talk about
male and female coming together? Being compatible? Because all
we're going to be trying to do is find somebody that fits our
programming" ~ **Siayoum Atum Ab Ankh Rhem**

The Ankh Life: The Mathematics of Sex Part 3 by Anthos
El Ma'at Ra

'Women are feeling insecure on the planet overall... as if good
sex is not a part of the life of struggle, pain, aggravation, and
frustration with men that she was taught to expect. She has guilt
about being happy and satisfied in any given moment, or for too
long a period of time. In essence she does not know how to receive
or why she should receive.

Okay you know I can't leave the masculine mind out, ladies
let's be honest the men too have to be in balance with your energy,
so how you would with his. So below I share a short piece for the
men, as men are usually active and ready to ENTER THE
COURSE (INTER -COURSE), but with proper discipline on both
of you guys part he can control his over drive to be disciplined by
his Goddess.

Here is something I knew all along but barely knew it really
made a difference: Verbal Penis Worship is very effective......
WOW!! Honestly, this is something that women have done in their
thoughts or after being with a wonderful man. Verbal Penis
Worship sounds like this: "Girl, let me tell you, his penis is
beautiful and so majestic, his head was perfect, the curve was
amazing, I could feel all of him...."

Men enjoy being worshiped verbally, so maybe it's time
women made this a regular practice in their cosmic evolution. A
friend of mine said he had a girl tell him his "penis is so beautiful"
when he was a teen. Still today when he has a bad day he thinks of

114

that moment and smiles….. We have been conditioned in this society to hide any feeling of appreciation towards our sexual organs. It is a shame we can't express our gratitude to these organs of creation and inspiration. Do you know in some parts of the world there are festivals that worship the penis? A whole day or days of chanting partying and enjoying the organ of males. Groups such as Hinduism, show a Goddess Shiva on top Kali's Lingam. Japan has a shrine and festival dedicated to Manhood, the Mara Kannon Shrine. In Egypt Min is the ancient God of fertility, always shown with an erection of course!

Adoring and loving each other's creative organs should definitely be part of love making. Here are some ways you can boost your man's penis ego by worshiping his penis verbally. He will definitely thank you and he will feel like a million bucks.

Kneeling Goddess:

Do this before love making, greet his penis with your first impression. Kneeling in front of your King, get close to his sacred mound and adore it with words, touch, and kisses – even through the pants. Treat his penis as separate from the man; speak to it as if it is its own entity (it does have a mind of its own sometimes lol). Use kindness, honesty and be real with him. Adore his penis with words and light touch.

Fellatio:

Of course fellatio is a good way to worship any man. Please be in the moment, take his cues, look into his eyes, enjoy the act of sucking, after all you are doing the worshiping so come with your full self here just as you'd want his full self in his worship of you.

Some words you can use:
"it's beautiful"
"amazing can I kiss it"
"Wow. Just how I imagined it – your greatness"
"I can't wait to feel you in me"

"am I dreaming, pinch me"
"my mouth is watering"
"you have a nice strong helmet"
"it smells, tastes delicious"
"I praise the head of my King, sweet nectar that comes from within"

Love:

Above all, men crave love. Most men are painfully aware of their imperfections and deep down may not believe they deserve to be loved. So finding a woman who can make them feel loved and deserving of love can satisfy a deep unspoken craving.

2. They may not realize how much they need to be loved until they actually experience genuine mature love.

3. It may take them a while to differentiate between *love* and *sex*.

4. In a mature relationship, each party contributes to the emotional security of the other by satisfying these cravings.

5. All relationships have ups and downs. All individuals have imperfections and annoying habits. It is the *emotional support* that makes it worthwhile to preserve a relationship through the many challenges.

Though we know what happens physically to men and women during orgasm (muscle contractions, increased heart rate, and movement of the uterus and vagina), the real feeling of climax comes from a number of chemical reactions in our body as I describe above, through much discipline together as one cosmic union you can target these parts of the body to become much vibrant in your cosmic evolution.

If you want him to strive to become a better husband and a better man because of his love for you... Through the over standing of this cosmic guide, both man and woman will learn and inner stand the mathematics of sex. This now brings me to the core

116

of this Cosmic guide: What has Mathematics got to do with Sex? Actually, a lot. Physical attraction depends on ratio. Our attraction to another person's body increases if that body is symmetrical and in proportion. Likewise, if a face is in proportion, we are more likely to notice it and find her beautiful.

In The Golden Ratio (or Golden Section-"Sex-on") is based on Fibonacci Numbers, where every number in the sequence (after the second) is the sum of the previous 2 numbers: "1, 1, 2, 3, 5, 8, 13, 21, ..."

You are a template of this Golden Ratio from Creation, just like many of you have found your Twin Flames. The proportion of the length of your love, the position of your InterSex Bodies, and the Vibration of your Soul Connection all conform to some aspect of the Golden Ratio.

When your Twin Flame is in union with your self, there is a Cosmic balance proportion to both Souls. You are the Mathematics of Sex and Cosmic Love.

This is the MATHEMATICS OF SEX, embrace your evolution through the Sacred Geometry of Sex!

~ Anthos El Ma'at Ra

Welcome to my Maths Class

"The speed limit for Sex is 68, many have broken the Law's in overdrive to 69, don't be lame, Cosmic Love is the name of the game so you better Teach her 69 tricks, don't be interrupted by her period that's 6.9 Usain Bolt world record shit...
Let me explain with my mathematics brain ...
Two horizontal angles can't INTER-SECT(ENTER-SEX),
Male and Female that's cosmic math 101 did you get this lesson yet. let me go a bit deeper, Men you better wake up an inner stand the mathematics of your Goddess, before you ADD the bed make sure you surrender your mind to her, don't MINUS her clothes if you not sure to put a ring on her finger, if you DIVIDE her legs you better be ready to be her Man, that's real G-Shit, so you have SUBTRACTED her draws and still don't' want to commit, so Ladies get that fool off you before he SQUARE ROOT your ass, cause he cheating with his lame ass mathematics. Am Out" ~ Anthos El Ma'at Ra

The Ankh Life: "Welcome to my Maths Class" (Men)

"...Men you better wake up and inner stand the mathematics of your Goddess, before you ADD the bed make sure you surrender your mind to her, don't MINUS her clothes if you not sure to put a ring on it, if you DIVIDE her legs you better be ready to be her Man, that's real G-Shit, so you have SUBTRACT her draws and still don't want to commit, so Ladies get that fool off you before he SQUARE ROOT your ass, cause he cheating with lame ass mathematics." Am Out

Wisdom: "Men if you need your women to inner stand Cosmic Love, try not turn her into a Christian, if you want to worship her don't have her become a Muslim, and if you so in need of a Heaven, become conscious of you and her and study the principles of her Divine Energy... She will bring peace on Earth to her King... she's your Goddess... and that's Cosmic Love in Mathematics"

~ Tony Huggup aka **Anthos El Ma'at Ra**, author of The *Ankh Life: Children of the Hidden Seeds*

There are different levels to sex. Think of it as a ladder: you should be able to go up and down the ladder, from the lowest chakra of base lust to the highest chakra of pure, spiritual love, and the balance is somewhere in between (that's how my Spirit Guides explained it to me). It's not wrong to want to just 'fuck' sometimes, but if you are only ever operating on the lower four chakras, you are missing out on experiencing the higher spiritual aspect of love-making.

"When the man is doing what he's supposed to be doing right (and it's not all about ejaculation it's about orgasm - men orgasm too). When a man stays in tune with himself he allows the woman to have a firm, steady place so she can fly off and go wherever she wants to go...she's riding the waves – he's supposed to stay present (I asked "so the man's not supposed to orgasm?") No. Orgasm is different to ejaculation. When a man ejaculates that it, over, done. When he's having an orgasm he's allowing the waves of energy, the current, to flow through him, and as it's flowing through, it's clearing blocks. (Orgasm means to expand)" ~ *Siayoum* **Atum Ab Ankh Rhem**

Make it your goal to not just want to get the ring on your finger, but to experience the highest, purest form of Love – which starts with loving your SELF.

****

A Black Womans Beatitudes

TAL Book of Wisdom 45:10

Blessed are the Black Men who put a Ring on It:

for theirs is the Kingdom of the Black Womans Yoni,

Blessed are those Black Men who yearns for his Queen:

for they will be comforted,

Blessed are the Black Men who seek for his Queen:

for she shall bring him peace,

Blessed are the Black Men who hunger and thirst for his Queen:

for he will be satisfied,

Blessed are the Black Men who shows Unconditional Love:

for he has his Queens's Loyalty

Blessed are the Black Men who keep it real:

for they will have respect from their Queens,

Blessed are the Black Men who never lay a hand on his Black Woman:

for they will be called Role Models,

Blessed are those Black Men who strive to have a foundation:

for there will he always find his Black Queen.

For Her Black Man

~ Evil Prevails when a Good Man Fails to Act. ~ Anthos El Ma'at Ra   ANKH

Did you Get the Ring On Your Finger?

"Times have changed so much that Marriage is no longer a Foundation within this Society. The Songs that used to make you rock away and dance every day no longer play on the radio. All the TV Shows depict women as Ruthless or Docile Hoes Bitches Sluts and the men as Pimps Players Thugs Men obsessed with their Jobs and Sex Etc.
*But have no fear Ladies there are still some Knights with Shining Armour, some Mandingo Warriors and Messengers from God and Men there are some Divine Goddess that Smell just like Sunflowers with Amazing Powers like Beautiful Lotus Flowers..."~ **Kushi Myers***

If you have followed this guide to the T and completed the 6 Month Test, you should both be happily on your way to planning your wedding. If not, ask your Self the following questions;

- Did I give up the coochie too quickly?

- Did I make it clear to him from the beginning what I wanted from the relationship?

- Did we follow the Plan?

- Did we decide that the ring is not the most important thing in our relationship as a Spiritual Union?

Marriage is Not the Be All and End All!

If you succeeded in getting the ring on your finger…now what?

My good friend Bunmi (I could even go so far as to call him my *best* friend), a fine Nigerian brother who I've known for over 20 years has been married twice; once to a Jamaican, and then to an African woman. He had this to say;

"Some women change once they get the ring on their finger, as if to say "I've got him now, I don't need to make an effort anymore". When dating, some women make the effort to look prim and proper but once married start going to bed with any old wrapper on their head. In Africa, women are trained from little girls how to adorn themselves for their husband and how to keep him focused on her; what perfumes to wear, how to look good all the time. They know the way to keep a man in the house is with good food. It is very rare to find an African woman who cannot cook. Also, a woman must know how to respect her man. If he

*sees she is 'submissive' (e.g. not raising her voice at him,
especially in front of his friends) he is more inclined to commit to
her. Submission is not a bad word. It is the woman's natural
desire to want to be submissive to her man".*

I actually agree with his last statement, although a lot of you
may not. In my poem **'R U The One?'**, I asked *"...Can you make
me submit to you? Not through force, but willingly, because you
are submitted to the Almighty..."*

See I believe a woman will *willingly* submit to a man if he proves
himself *worthy* of being submitted to.

Remember your role in the relationship as the woman, and
allow him to play his as the man. Men are not likely to put a ring
on a woman who won't submit to them.

I'm sorry if you've got to the end of this book and you're
disappointed because there's no 'magic formula' to getting the
ring on your finger. But if you are prepared to do the WORK
(both inner and with your partner when he shows up) you will
stand a much better chance of getting the ring on your finger.

Wishing you an abundance of Love, Happiness, Peace and
Harmony on your Love Quest, and remember, it starts with loving
your SELF!

Cezanne

****

Summary

So to conclude this book, I will sum it up:

1. Get to know your SELF before seeking to get to know someone else

2. Know your worth; Love and Respect your Self, then you will *command* Love and Respect from others.

3. Identify your issues and work on your Self so that you are the best version of your Self that you can be. Complete a Self-development program.

4. Learn your her-story; are you suffering from Post Traumatic Slave Syndrome? (Do you have any of the symptoms?)

5. Are you still carrying Emotional Baggage from past relationships? Heal Your Self! Go into the relationship as a whole person, not a half person trying to make a whole

6. You are not a victim! Men know their boundaries but will break them if you allow them to

7. You Attract What You Are: BE the Love that you are seeking to attract

8. Know your Power; Get in touch with your Femininity; Trust your Intuition

9. Know What you Want; don't settle for less

10. Are you Ready for Love? Start putting it 'out there'

11. Write the Vision, make it Plain (be realistic)

12. Focus on Your Desires; do your Daily Visualisation

13. Prepare your Self – Clear out the clutter of past relationships!

14. Attend events where you are likely to meet a 'Good Black Man' e.g. Cultural events, Black cinema clubs, Book signing events, live performance events, evening classes

15. Be Open to the Abundance of the Universe!

16. Have a Plan; don't give up the coochie too quickly if your plan is to get married

17. Do the 'DIY Arranged Marriage' for the best chances of dating success

18. Learn the Afrocentric way of a spiritual union, rather than the Eurocentric way of a (physical) union.

19. Let him be the man in the relationship (even if he's earning less than you). Practice operating in your Feminine Energy and allowing him to operate in his Masculine Energy. Learn all you can about the Afrocentric perspective on Love & Marriage as opposed to the Eurocentric

20. Understand the Creative Power of your Womb, and learn the Science of Black Male and Female Sex

21. Marriage is not the Be All and End All!

How Do You Keep Love Alive?

Getting the ring on your finger is one thing, *sustaining* the relationship is another!

In the follow-up to this book, I'll be interviewing Black couples who have been together for at least 10 years to advise YOU on how to sustain *your* relationship!

Remember:

BLACK LOVE = BLACK POWER
We Belong Together!

****

Poetry from the Brothers to the Black Woman

You are...Part 1 by Kwame McPherson

...my inspiration

The cornerstone of my focus

A part of my concentration

Undiluted, pure

Attaining a higher self

A mystical vibration

...my proclamation

A vocal veneer

A vibrant visualisation

Pronouncing, announcing

A uniqueness of strength

Steeped in years of determination

An eternal continuation

...my exclamation

Heart skips a beat,

A mouth-watering manifestation

A yearning, wanting, longing

Loins burning, stomach churning

Make love until early morning

A new type of dawning

...mesmerising

Tantalising, satisfying, gratifying
Every cell in my body
I'm not lying
Straining, staining, holding
My being in a grip
Factualising, justifying, simplifying
How to be
How not to slip

...captivating
Joining, uniting, aligning
Grasping my soul
Enhancing my meditation
Flowing through my veins
A sensuous, sweet, sensation

...my compulsion
Pushing, pulling
Trying, guiding
Taking, leading
Believing yet feeling
Visioning, dreaming
Promoting, seeing
Our potential
Our spiritual meaning

...my motivation

Challenging me to see

Enhancing all I'm destined to be

Walking beside

A satisfaction

A counteraction

A people's continuation

…my construction

Helping us to build

Our foundation

Captured from an Ancestral tradition

Blessed by Our Creators personal function

A positive capitalisation

A consistent, constant captivation

…my completion

Fulfilling a journey

Towards our destination

A walk

A trip

An excursion

Blessed

Taking us to our spiritual conclusion

Written on a vibe, by Kwame M.A. McPherson, 28th December 2008.

Available in *'The Love Poems'*,
www.lulu.com/spotlight/maxkey

You Are...Part 2

...the honey in my Cerassie tea

...the Ackee with my Saltfish

...the Rum in my Coke

...the Ganja in my cake, well soaked

...the Hummingbird in my Hibiscus

Touching me here, there

Gently touching everywhere

...the ray of sunshine

Smiling that beautiful smile

To say you're all mine

...Dunn's River Falls

Flowing, feeling all parts of me

From the bush to the warm Caribbean Sea

Filling my vessel for me to be

...a fine fit female with two bumpsious mounds

A reminder of Jackfruit

Full, firm round

A mouthful at any one time

One part stiff

Yet delicious, tasty like wash – sugar, water and lime

...the rich, green fields of sugar cane

Its sap sweet, tasty rich
Sucking its juices
So much energy for me to gain

...the delicious Julie mango
Dripping fluids
Licked by my lips already set
My tongue soft tasting, wet

...Soursop
Spongy, supple, slushy
Waiting on my banana to make it even more mushy

...my Blue Draws
Covered in banana leaf
Baked in the ground
Like your legs wrapped around
The heat in between so profound

...my Rice and Peas
Spiced in Coconut Milk
Scelion, never cooked with cheese
Tasting your lips is like touching my skin to silk

...my marinated jerk
Succulent, flavoured a tasty dish
My stomach never filled like this

My soul now complete
My total, ultimate wish

...my boiled up Cho-cho
Steamed, sexy, scrumptious,
Licking my lips there's a happy smile
Far from a frown
Because the look of the Cho-cho
Show me what to expect
When we touch the bed
Just me and you

...my Guiness Punch
A warm, soothing drink during lunch
Growing within
I feel your touch the taste making my head spin

...curried chicken back
Moving all the way down
Gently touching my insides
From my neck to my butt crack

...Hot Pepper Pot Soup
Exciting my body, my soul
Your Scotch-bonnet burning like the sun
Capturing my heart, making me whole
Being with you is fun

Like when we're in the Caribbean or Africa, it just cannot done!

Written on a vibe, by Kwame M.A. McPherson, 28th December 2008.

Available in '*The Love Poems*',
www.lulu.com/spotlight/maxkey

Your Heart is Lighter than a Feather
Or a Billion Ants Eating a
Piece of Sweet Watermelon Together
We know that this is what you Do
You are a 100 Percent Proof of Living Divine Truth
And we all want to Step in your World
And Walk in your Divine Shoes just Smiling
While Thinking out Loud in Bright Shiny Ultraviolet
And a Sudden outburst of Laughter
While being Absolutely Silent
Your Beautiful Mind is like your own Private Island
Where Everything is Everything from
Powerful Energy to the Songs that Colorful Birds Sing
And Delicious Health Foods and Sacred Sabbaticals
Nano Molecules while we all are just Loving You
Your Cup is always Running Over
Carrying all of Humanity on Both of your Shoulders
You are The Next Level of
Existence as Mother Earth gets Older
You're the Bomb exactly like Crazy Calm
Or a Jade Quartz Elephant in a Quite Storm
You are a Dynamic Reaction
To All the Laws of Attraction
Soul to Sole And even Old Fashioned but Always Fantastic
You Make all of us Believe in Magic
By Defying the Laws of Gravity Flying like a Hawk
When ever we are Apart
We Call on God to Bless our Kidneys and Heart
We become Prayer Warriors that Constantly
Meditate and Channel Supreme Thoughts

And Walking just like the Ancient Egyptians Walked
And the Last thing I want to say from my Heart is that
The Legend Must be True
Because You have a PHD In Miracles

© Kushi Myer

The Black Woman

We were identified by our spine,
the black woman and I,
a cord of togetherness,
not in negativity we reside.
A residue of purpose,
a method we embrace,
and once we knew this,
no other could replace.
We rang with intelligence,
sang in growth,
taught with spiritual guidance
learnt the lessons once told.
We are extra-ordinary people,
our minds are rare,
and through oppression we concurred
no longer biding with fear.

The Black Woman . . . . . .

We came out of her birth canal,
make love to her when she needs,
Take her hand and offer her a Godly home,
in prosperity we seek.
She doesn't suffer insomnia,
we offer her a liquor that's unique,
a fulfilling regiment of shut eye,
a comfortable chest to rest on when feeling fatigued.

She is our mother our daughter our wife,

She rejuvenates our soul through the thickness of strife,
We relax in her tenderness,
A priceless wake to her morning face rise,
An expression of truth she offers,
As we take her moist making it prime.
Her kindness is prevalent,
Out of a strong woman she has grown,
And only a man with strength can aspire,
As he makes her his primary goal,
Other men would shiver at the prospect,
Not realising the privilege,
Of being the black woman's husband,
Making her your wife an honourable gift.

This poem is for the Woman

For God Loved the World so Much

You are Exactly what She gave Us

With the Amazing Ability that can Always Save Us

No one Else in this Solar System Can do The Amazing things
Everyday Done by You

You are like a Beautiful Sunflower Growing in a Concrete Jungle

The Beautiful Sound of a Rain Forest Thunder

And that Good Feeling in the Pits of the Bottom of our Stomachs
that comes from it

Making the Coldest day of Winter

Feel like the Warmest Day of Summer

You don't need no Formal Introduction

So Here are your Divine Instruction

Live your Life to the Fullest as if Tomorrow Wasn't Loving it and
Always Enjoying it

Don't Say a Single Word because Your Energy and Vibration
and your Beautiful Smile will Always be Heard
Every Mid Night Afternoon and Morning
Give Praise to the Creator
And Prepare a Sacred Space to make a Shrine for your Ancestors
with a Beautiful Light
Sign a Love Letter and Send it on a Meteorite and Write
Something Divine that you Think
We would All Like Only you will know the Exact Time
when the time is Right
Connect with Every Beautiful Thing that Takes Flight
Repeat the Melodies
and Sing like the Red Mockingbirds Sings at Night
You are a Dynamic Perfect Being
Pieces of a Wonderful Divine Beautiful Dream
Always and Forever and Ever with Pure Love
For God Loved the World so Much
You are Exactly what She gave Us
© Kushi Myer

Beloved Black Women

We are but shadows to support your substance
This is not romanticism affectation for advantage
This is the Law of light, shadows, substance.
Be yourself in the light,
the shadow is compelled to follow you
It depends on you for life not the other way around.
© Vidal Montgomery

IMMA DO FOR YOU

I'm about to open the door for you cause you are a special lady

Imma wait till you walk through,

I have a rose in my hand I'm gonna present to you

I hope you like it too,

I have a ring in my pocket I'm gonna give to you

And ask you to marry me for you are my lady empress and queen

I booked a table for 2 so we can eat and drink till the night falls through

I booked a hotel room for if you get tired too

And so much more that comes straight from the heart from me to you.

Imma do for you what a man should do

Imma hold you, kiss you, caress you, care for you and love you

From me to you.

Written BY DA TRUTH (Majah Tunda, FB)

I saw her clearly
looking at me softly
her lips soft and pinkish tasting of undiluted honey
her smile lightening up the room like the glow of the sun
her face oval, with clear dark brown eyes
her voice tinkling clear and soft like that of a dove
her figure moderately slim and shapely
she had the intellect of a goddess
she said to me "I am all yours"
I reached for her hand but she left in a mist
leaving her subtle scent to reck my senses
I am longing for her
My twin flame. ~ Anthos El Ma'at Ra

Twin Flame

I saw her clearly

Looking at me softly

Her lips soft and pinkish tasting of undiluted honey

Her smile lighting up the room like the glow of the sun

Her face oval, with clear dark brown eyes

Her voice tinkling clear and soft like that of a dove

Her figure moderately slim and shapely

She had the intellect of a goddess

She said to me "I am all yours"

I reached for her hand but she left in a mist

Leaving her subtle scent to wreck my senses

I am longing for her,

My twin flame

~ Anthos El Ma'at Ra

The following poem was written by my Higher Self, on behalf of The Black Woman to the Black Man, and is partly inspired by the book: *'An Afrocentric Guide to a Spiritual Union'* by Ra Un Nefer Amen;

R U 'The One'?

Are you The One?
Can you make my heart *beat* like an African drum?
(du-dum, du-dum, du-dum)

Are you the star I've been hoping, wishing and praying upon?

Is it *you* sending *me* positive vibrations
Letting me know that *I'm* The One?

Do you love me, the Black Woman
And will you put me on a pedestal, where I beong?
Will you hold me in high esteem,
And treat me like a Queen?

Can I look up to *you*
And give you the respect you want from me;
Do you conduct yourself with honesty, dignity and integrity?

Are you The One?

Are you my soul mate,
The One with whom I can share a deep spiritual connection
Are you looking for True Love, or just a one night stand?

C'mon, can we talk freely?
And will you open up to me completely
Because communication is the key...
Can you relate to me?
I am a spiritual being having an earth experience
And I'd like to experience something with *you*
What would it be? It would be like a fire ignited,
Two souls from a past life, finally re-united!
You are the object of my desire, but I don't know,
Can you take me to my highest heights and then,
can we go a little... higher?

See, I'm seeking The One who experiences a *natural* high
through Prayers and Meditation,
Who operates on a higher spiritual vibration,
Connecting with the Mother/Father of all creation...

Are you 'The One'?

You are my brother and a King,
So don't deny me my rightful position as your Queen
I'M the one you need,

No other race can take my place,
I am your spiritual and intellectual equal!
Hmm...I don't even know if you're The One,
Maybe you're just a figment of my imagination...

But,

Can we tune our thoughts in synchrony,
Two becoming One Mind, as in the great Marriage Mystery
For what God joins together no one can come between...
Yes, I'm looking for my husband!
Someone who'll treat me the way I deserve to be...

Are you 'The One'?

Can you make me submit to you?
Not through force, but willingly
Because you are submitted to the Almighty?
Because then, I will give you the respect you deserve,
Honouring you and treating you like a King
(your throne being our home)
Can we live together in unity;
Perfect Love, Perfect Peace
Perfect Harmony?

Yes, I'm looking for my King!
Someone who takes pride in;
Him Self, his culture, his his-story
Who's not ashamed of his Black-identity;

Are you 'The One'?

Do you know your history?
Are you mentally free?
Do you know where you're coming from?
Are you like a tree, standing strong?
You must know these things
For you to be 'The One'.

Because if you're The One,
Then maybe I can be The One *you* can depend on,
The One you can trust and lean on?
I will nurture you into YOUR unfolding
I will love holding you in my arms
I will caress you, cherish you, treasure you,
Like a rare diamond found in Ancient Kemet
And brought to this land where no price could be put on it
Yes, I will treasure you and polish you daily
Until those rough edges become smooth...
And then,
I will support you - emotionally
Helping you achieve all your dreams
I won't hurt you, mistreat you, disrespect you,
At least, not unless you give me reason to...(Selah)

I will give to you Selflessly,
Seeking nothing in return
I will love you unconditionally
And together we will be an immutable Force
Which nothing can come between
(Except of course God, Who is our Source)

You will be my Sun and I will be your Moon,
And we can feed off each other's energy
Spreading Love to our community
And sharing our good fortune...

Now I know this is a tall order,
But brothers, if you think you fit the position
Then show me by the raising of your hand –
That is, ONLY if you're 'The One'!

© Cezanne 2009

(on the '*Seeds of Love*' CD available to download from
www.reverbnation.com/cezannepoetess)

Acknowledgements

First I want to thank the Great Creator, my Higher Self and my Spirit Guides for the idea to write this book, the idea to ask the brothers to contribute to it, and for allowing the inspiration to flow freely through me as I wrote it, and for everything 'coming together' in such a short space of time!

Next, I would like to give special "Thankh You" on behalf of my Sistars/Queens, to my Brothers/Kings for their contributions namely:

Nigel Beckles, Reflections On Relationships (FB Group)

Kwame McPherson www.kwamemcpherson.com

Darren Moxam www.darrenmoxam.com

Michael Baisden, New York Times Bestselling Author & Motivational Speaker: (FB)

Siayoum Atum Ab Ankh Rhem, Astrologer

Orman Griffith (FB)

Michael, BIS Publications www.bispublications.co.uk

Toyin Agbetu, Ligali www.ligali.org

Kushi Myers www.smashwords.com/books/view/269601

Wilfred 'Rawventure' Campbell (FB)

Tony Huggup aka **Anthos El Ma'at Ra**, Author of 'The Ankh Life' Follow him on Twitter: @TheAnkhLife

Jide Oriogun aka **Knee Deep**: Black Cinema Club http://meetup.com/Black-Cinema-Club, www.colourfulradio.com

Matsinhe, The Mella Center www.mellacenter.co.uk

Wadada Stanbury, Saxophonist (FB)

Vidal Montgomery, Professional Double Bass player (FB)

Kolade, Learn Yoruba in London (FB Group)

Carl Foster, Author of Selfmade www.selfmade.me.uk

Garry Grant, Entrepreneur (FB)

Jak Beula (Nubian Jak) www.nubianjak.com

Dennis Brown, Amelu Arts www.ameluarts.com

Edward Ofosu, Artist

Rudolph Mendoza, sculptor

Clarence Davies aka Freestyle www.colourfulradio.com

Minty, Nubia House Radio www.nubiahousemedia.com

Also Tau RA (FB), Eye'm King (FB), Da Truth aka Majah Tunder (FB) Trevor Richardson, Morpheus Prime (Google +), Bunmi O'Tuminu, LG, Yeshuah the 1st, Alex Burnett, Brian Quavar, Byron Deslandes, and Jaiyeola Bagbansoro – thank you all, without your contributions this book wouldn't be what it is!

About Cezanne

I am a Self-taught Visual and Spoken Word artist and Self-published Author, guided by my in-tuition.

I am an Evolutionary Entrepreneur; meaning I help people to grow spiritually through my art, poetry and Self-help books.

In 2007 I reached a point in my Christian walk where I began to question everything I'd been taught to believe, so I asked God for 'the Truth'. This marked a turning-point in my spiritual journey; everything I've learnt since then, I've shared in my Self-help novel *'Single, Spiritual...AND Sexual!'* (paperback first published in December 2012). For full details and to read Year One FREE visit **www.singlespiritualandsexual.com**

Between 2009-10 I learnt how to meditate and in the process I painted 11 paintings; I hadn't painted in over 20 years and never with oils on canvas before! You can learn more about the **Colour Therapy & Symbolism** used in my paintings on the Art Page of my blog: **www.cezannepoetess.com**

In June 2013 I published the Book of Lyrics to my debut poetry CD *'Seeds of Love'* which compliments my Self-help novel (all 13 poems on the CD feature in the story). To listen to/download the album visit **www.reverbnation.com/cezannepoetess**.

I am committed to providing platforms for Black Singles and Couples to meet and discuss the issues that we face in our relationships, and to work towards building sustainable relationships. After the success of two events I organised in 2010 **'What Black Men Want'** and **What Black Women Need'** I have decided to use future Book-signing events I organise as platforms for us to meet, discuss issues that affect our relationships/community, and to learn how to heal ourselves/our relationships. For details of my Book-signing events visit **www.singlespiritualandsexual.com/Book Signing Events.**

Join my Facebook Group: **Sustainable Black Relationships**

'Follow' my blog to receive email updates about my activities: **www.cezannepoetess.com**

Please Leave a Review!

Did you enjoy reading this book? I 'pushed this baby out' in six weeks as I wanted to finish it before I make my Sankofa journey to Ghana to do the research for my next book! The hardest part was getting all the contributions to fit with each other and into what I was already saying; it was a bit like putting together a giant jigsaw puzzle! I'm not saying I got it right first time, so if you can see any ways I can make it better, do let me know! All constructive criticism greatly appreciated! I look forward to reading your feedback...

Please leave your Customer Review at: **www.lulu.com (Search: Cezanne Poetess)**

Lightning Source UK Ltd.
Milton Keynes UK
UKOW03f0634310814

237817UK00011B/113/P